Illustration: Magali Lefrançois.

Louis Riel, 1844–1885

Sharon Stewart

Sharon Stewart has written seven books for young readers: *The Minstrel Boy* (1997), *The Dark Tower* (1998), *Spider's Web* (1998), *My Anastasia* (1999), *City of the Dead* (2001), *Raven Quest* (2003), and *Banished from Our Home* (2004). Several of her books have been translated into French and other languages. She has been shortlisted for a number of awards, including the Geoffrey Bilson Award for Historical Fiction, and in 2005 her novel *Raven Quest* won the Ontario Library Association's Silver Birch Award.

Sharon Stewart is also a professional editor who works as a freelancer in educational publishing. She specializes in language arts and social studies. She studied history at Simon Fraser University, the University of London (England), and the University of Toronto, and has a Master's degree in French colonial history. She has taught English as a Foreign Language in Harbin, China. She is married to Roderick Stewart, the author of several books on Norman Bethune and of *Wilfrid Laurier: A Pledge for Canada* in the Quest Library. They currently live in Richmond Hill, Ontario.

In the same collection

Ven Begamudré, *Isaac Brock: Larger Than Life*.

Lynne Bowen, *Robert Dunsmuir: Laird of the Mines*.

Kate Braid, *Emily Carr: Rebel Artist*.

Kathryn Bridge, *Phyllis Munday: Mountaineer*.

William Chalmers, *George Mercer Dawson: Geologist, Scientist, Explorer*.

Anne Cimon, *Susanna Moodie: Pioneer Author*.

Deborah Cowley, *Lucille Teasdale: Doctor of Courage*.

Gary Evans, *John Grierson: Trailblazer of Documentary Film*.

Judith Fitzgerald, *Marshall McLuhan: Wise Guy*.

lian goodall, *William Lyon Mackenzie King: Dreams and Shadows*.

Stephen Eaton Hume, *Frederick Banting: Hero, Healer, Artist*.

Naïm Kattan, *A.M. Klein: Poet and Prophet*.

Betty Keller, *Pauline Johnson: First Aboriginal Voice of Canada*.

Heather Kirk, *Mazo de la Roche: Rich and Famous Writer*.

Michelle Labrèche-Larouche, *Emma Albani: International Star*.

Wayne Larsen, *A.Y. Jackson: A Love for the Land*.

Francine Legaré, *Samuel de Champlain: Father of New France*.

Margaret Macpherson, *Nellie McClung: Voice for the Voiceless*.

Dave Margoshes, *Tommy Douglas: Building the New Society*.

Marguerite Paulin, *René Lévesque: Charismatic Leader*.

Marguerite Paulin, *Maurice Duplessis: Powerbroker, Politician*.

Raymond Plante, *Jacques Plante: Behind the Mask*.

T.F. Rigelhof, *George Grant: Redefining Canada*.

Tom Shardlow, *David Thompson: A Trail by Stars*.

Arthur Slade, *John Diefenbaker: An Appointment with Destiny*.

Roderick Stewart, *Wilfrid Laurier: A Pledge for Canada*.

André Vanasse, *Gabrielle Roy: A Passion for Writing*.

John Wilson, *John Franklin: Traveller on Undiscovered Seas*.

John Wilson, *Norman Bethune: A Life of Passionate Conviction*.

Rachel Wyatt, *Agnes Macphail: Champion of the Underdog*.

Louis Riel

**Bibliothèque et Archives nationales du Québec and
Library and Archives Canada Cataloguing In Publication**
Stewart, Sharon (Sharon Roberta), 1944-

    Louis Riel : firebrand

    (The quest library ; 31)
    Includes bibliographical references and index.

    ISBN 978-1-894852-26-5

    1. Riel, Louis, 1844-1885. 2. Riel Rebellion, 1885. 3. Red River Rebellion, 1869-1870. 4. Métis - Prairie Provinces - Biography. I. Title. II. Series: Quest library ; 31.
FC3217.1.R53S73 2007   971.05'1092   C2007-940826-5

Legal Deposit: Second quarter 2007
Library and Archives Canada
Bibliothèque et Archives nationales du Québec

XYZ Publishing acknowledges the support of The Quest Library project by the Book Publishing Industry Development Program (BPIDP) of the Department of Canadian Heritage. The opinions expressed do not necessarily reflect the views of the Government of Canada.

The publishers further acknowledge the financial support our publishing program receives from The Canada Council for the Arts, the ministère de la Culture et des Communications du Québec, and the Société de développement des entreprises culturelles.

Chronology: Rhonda Bailey
Index: Darcy Dunton
Layout: Édiscript enr.
Cover design: Zirval Design
Cover illustration: Magali Lefrançois
Photo research: Sharon Stewart and Rhonda Bailey

 Printed and bound in Canada by Lebonfon
(Val-d'or, Québec, Canada) in May 2007.

XYZ Publishing
1781 Saint Hubert Street
Montreal, Quebec H2L 3Z1
Tel: (514) 525-2170
Fax: (514) 525-7537
E-mail: info@xyzedit.qc.ca
Website: www.xyzedit.qc.ca

Distributed by: University of Toronto Press Distribution
5201 Dufferin Street
Toronto, ON, M3H 5T8
Tel: 416-667-7791; Toll-free: 800-565-9523
Fax: 416-667-7832; Toll-free: 800-221-9985
E-mail: utpbooks@utpress.utoronto.ca
Website: utpress.utoronto.ca

International Rights: Contact André Vanasse, tel. (514) 525-2170 # 25
E-mail: andre.vanasse@xyzedit.qc.ca

SHARON STEWART

RIEL

Louis

FIREBRAND

XYZ
Publishing

To Roderick, for all the reasons.

Contents

Prologue: The Chain   1

Part One: Flint and Steel
 1 Son of a Métis Hero   7
 2 Into the World   15
 3 Who Will Lead Our People?   29

Part Two: Blaze
 4 Loyal Subject of Her Majesty   41
 5 Resistance   51
 6 Father of a Province   65

Part Three: Embers
 7 Dispossessed and Exiled   77
 8 Prophet of the New World   93
 9 Wanderer   103

Part Four: Wildfire
 10 Uprising   121
 11 Trials   137

Epilogue: The Legacy   153

Chronology of
Louis Riel (1844-1885)   159
Sources Consulted   185
Index   188

Acknowledgments

I would like to thank Dr. Philippe Mailhot of the St. Boniface Museum for reading this manuscript and for his help with the "howlers." Any errors remaining are the responsibility of the author.

A Métis rider, dashing and bold.
He is guiding a Red River cart train.

Prologue

The Chain

A party of Métis horsemen rode pell-mell into the yard of the Riel farm on River Road and reined in hard, wheeling their horses.

"Louis! The surveyors from Canada are on Monsieur Marion's land!" The voice belonged to André Nault.

A young man with a mane of curly hair froze with his hand on the bridle of the horse he was leading. His dark, deep-set eyes flashed as he stared at his cousin. "Where? You saw them yourself?" he demanded.

"*Mais oui!* On the Marions' hay privilege. About an hour ago now!" André's voice was shrill. "I was with our herd and the Canadians showed up with sextants and chains and survey stakes. I told them they have no right to survey Métis land, but they paid no heed!"

Louis swung into the saddle. "Of course they didn't," he replied. "The dolts don't understand French. But we'll soon set them straight!"

The hooves of their horses drummed an urgent tattoo on the frozen earth as they galloped toward the Marion farm. The air rushing past Louis's face was cold, but his cheeks were flushed with excitement. Now the moment of confrontation had come, and his whole life seemed a preparation for it.

The date was October 11, 1869. Though snow had not yet fallen, the day was gloomy and chill. For months now, tension had been building in the colony of Red River. Since late April, people there had known that the Hudson's Bay Company had sold the whole colony, lock, stock, and barrel to the new Dominion of Canada. Rumours had begun to circulate that people might lose their land under the new arrangement. For although some settlers held title under the Hudson's Bay Company to the lands they farmed, many had worked their fields for as much as forty years with no title at all. The local First Nations people, the Saulteaux, were concerned too. How would their original title to the land be extinguished? Might not all lands now be handed over to newcomers from Canada, and the original inhabitants left with nothing? Worst of all, not a word had come from the Dominion of Canada to explain its plans for the future or to calm people's fears.

Folk complained and muttered about their rights, and nobody more than the Métis, the largest group in the Red River Colony. The descendants of French-Canadian voyageurs and First Nations women, the

Métis had hunted buffalo and worked for the great fur-trading companies for generations, meanwhile farming long, narrow river lots in the settlement. By now, the most prosperous among them owned freighting operations and traded in the local grain market. All Métis knew that they would have much to lose if Red River was taken over by a horde of English-speaking land-grabbers from Canada. So they watched events with narrowed eyes. Then, in late August, a Canadian survey party arrived to work in the settlement. The Métis warned the surveyors off their lands at Oak Point, southeast of Red River. Now, in October, the Canadians were meddling with their holdings again.

The Métis were superb riders, dashing and bold. As the group rode down on the survey party, the Canadians felt a thrill of fear, for the Métis had threatened them before. The horsemen encircled them, then dismounted, stepping close, then closer. The surveyors drew together defensively. A gust of cold wind lashed the dry prairie grass, and a fleeting shaft of sun broke through the scudding clouds, lighting up the men standing face to face.

Baptiste Tourond, a well-respected Métis, was with the group. So was Édouard Marion, who owned the land. But it was young Louis Riel who stepped forward to face Captain Webb, the man in charge of the survey.

"Stop!" Louis ordered, in clear English. "You will go no farther. This land belongs to Monsieur Marion. We will not allow the survey to continue."

"But I have orders – " blustered Captain Webb, his side-whiskers quivering with indignation.

Riel stared down at the hundred-link survey chain that lay stretched like a silvery snake upon the ground at his feet. Janvier Ritchot, standing beside him, followed his gaze. Grinning, the burly giant planted one big moccasined foot on the chain. Louis and the rest of the Métis followed suit and stared defiantly at the surveyors.

"There is nothing more for you to do here," Louis repeated. "Go! Now!"

Cowed and outnumbered, the surveyors packed their equipment. Louis watched them leave, exulting. We have won the first skirmish, he told himself, as the Métis cheered. He knew his people's resistance to Canada was just beginning. And he, Louis Riel, would lead them. He had found his mission.

Part One
Flint and Steel

Louis as a big-eyed boy in 1858, about the
time he travelled to Montreal to go to school.

1

Son of a Métis Hero

M any years earlier, a boy with tousled chestnut curls had stood hand in hand with his little sister beside a dusty cart track. They were waiting to see the first Métis hunting brigade of the year go by. They knew it was coming because they had heard the squealing of the ungreased axles of the carts all the way down by the Seine.

"Aren't they grand?" Louis cried, as the first Red River cart, drawn by plodding oxen, lumbered by. Sara squeezed his hand.

A rider on a prancing horse grinned down at them. He was splendid in his fringed and beaded buckskin and bright-coloured sash. *"Au revoir, mes petits!"* he called, sweeping off his wide-brimmed hat with a flourish.

"Au revoir, monsieur!" they chorused.

Cart after cart lumbered by, bound for the far West in search of the buffalo. It happened every year, in June and again in October.

"When they get back there'll be parties, with fiddle music and jigs," Louis told Sara. "But the best part is the stories about the hunt. And maybe they'll have to fight the Sioux. Oh, I wish I could go with them!"

But it wasn't likely that he ever would. Louis Riel was a Métis because his French-Canadian grandfather had married a woman of French and Chipewyan parentage. The Métis people shared the French language and the Catholic religion. But not all lived in the same way. Many earned a living by hunting buffalo. Some also traded goods to the United States in their Red River carts. Others manned the York boats and canoe brigades that carried the goods of the Hudson's Bay Company. But Louis's family belonged to the more settled, prosperous Métis of the Red River Settlement south of Lake Winnipeg. They owned a farm, and raised grain, vegetables, and livestock. His father, Jean-Louis Riel, also ran a gristmill on the Seine River. So it seemed likely that Louis's future would be the same.

∞

Louis's world was a place of riverside woods and farmland, with the open prairie rolling beyond. Gazing over the fields, he could see only church steeples and windmills poking above the horizon. There were just two really big buildings in Red River, and he knew both of them well. At the centre of the little settlement loomed the stone bastions of Upper Fort Garry, which belonged to the Hudson's Bay Company. The Company controlled trade and also the Council of Assiniboia, which governed the settlement. His father often went to the fort on business, and Louis tagged along. From there, gazing across the river, he could see the twin spires of the cathedral of St. Boniface soaring into the sky. He had been baptized in the cathedral, and attended mass there every Sunday.

Despite its small size, Red River was multicultural. The French Canadians and Métis were francophone and Catholic. The Saulteaux people spoke Cree, and some had been converted to the Protestant faith. Most of the anglophones were Protestants too. Some of them were English-speaking mixed-bloods, the children of Hudson's Bay Company traders and aboriginal women. Others were the descendants of Scottish settlers who had arrived in 1812, or of settlers who had arrived later from Upper Canada, later renamed Ontario.

Louis's father came to Red River around 1842 and bought a river lot next door to the Lagimodière family. Within months, he asked for the hand of pretty Julie Lagimodière. But although her parents were pleased, Julie hesitated. Not that Jean-Louis was not a good-looking fellow, and not that the French-Canadian Lagimodières objected to his being Métis, for they did not. But Julie did not wish to marry anybody. She wanted to be a nun.

In doubt about what she should do, she went to church one day to pray about her problem. On the way home, she suddenly felt herself enveloped in flames, yet she was not scorched. Looking up, she saw an old man in the clouds, "flashing with light, and encircled with fire."

"Disobedient child!" boomed a powerful voice. "Return home and tell your parents that you will obey them!"

Overcome with awe, Julie did as she was told. She and Jean-Louis were married in January, 1844. Louis Riel, the couple's first child, was born on October 22 of that year.

From the beginning, religion was part of the air Louis breathed. Julie hung over his cradle, murmuring prayers, and she and Jean-Louis vowed that the baby's first words were "Jesus," "Mary," and "Joseph." Soon he was old enough to learn to say the rosary, and to take part in family prayers each night. The Riels' next two children did not survive, so for four years, until the birth of Sara, Louis was not just an only son but a much-loved only child.

∞

His early life was full of excitement. When he was just five, his father played a starring role in a thrilling political drama. Métis and other local traders had long been challenging the Hudson's Bay Company law that all trade must go through the Company's post at Red River. To them, it made more sense to trade directly with the Americans, who paid higher prices. The more the Hudson's Bay Company tried to control the trade, the more the traders resisted. They also sent petitions against the Company to London.

In 1849, a Métis named Pierre-Guillaume Sayer was charged with illegal trafficking in furs. Crowds of angry Métis gathered at the courthouse and fired volleys of shots into the air. Their leader was Jean-Louis Riel. They had turned to him because he had confronted the Company before and was known as a fearless activist.

Now he and a group of Métis stormed into the courtroom.

"Free Sayer," demanded Jean-Louis, "or we'll set him free ourselves!"

In the end, Sayer was released, and his confiscated furs were returned to him.

"*Le commerce est libre! Vive la liberté!*" cheered the Métis. And they celebrated with a *feu de joie*, a happy crackle of gunfire.

Louis burned with excitement when he heard the news. "Papa is a hero, isn't he?" he demanded.

Julie Riel hugged him. "Yes, *mon petit chou*. He is helping our people," she told him.

The next big event came three years later, in the spring of 1852. The Red River flooded disastrously, sweeping away everything along its banks. Huddled with his family, soaked through and shivering, Louis watched the muddy, roiling waters engulf the family home.

"Does God *want* our house to be washed away?" he asked.

"Everything that happens is the will of God," replied his father.

In 1854, Jean-Louis borrowed funds and set up a gristmill on the Seine, which produced a modest living.

He built a bigger house, too. It was much needed, because more children had been born. After Sara, in 1848, had come Marie, in 1850, Octavie, in 1852, Eulalie, in 1853 and Charles, in 1854. Another son, Joseph, was born in 1857.

Louis, meanwhile, had grown into a handsome boy with big, thoughtful eyes. Wherever he went, Sara trotted at his heels, faithful as a shadow – part pet, part playmate. Together they played along the river near the mill, or in the woods and fields around their home. They must have had playmates from the Métis or First Nations communities too. The Riels and Lagimodières had strong roots in French Canada, and French was the language they taught their children, yet both Louis and Sara also became fluent in Cree.

Louis began school when he was seven years old. He first boarded at the convent school of the Grey Nuns in St. Boniface, and later attended the Christian Brothers' school, which was held in the library of the bishop's house. Already aware that some of his classmates had less than he did, Louis used to give his school lunch away to hungry children, until his mother found out and had him fed at school. No wonder some of the other boys saw him as a goody-goody.

One day, a schoolmate snatched his cap and threw it on the ground. "Fight, sissy," he jeered, cocking his fists.

Louis's face flushed scarlet. "Just you wait," he cried. "I shall ask my mother if it's all right to fight you. If she says yes, then we'll meet again."

He was a good student, and soon began to learn English and Latin. One day Bishop Alexandre-Antonin

Taché dropped in to see how the boys in the school were doing. He had known Louis all his life, and noticed him intent on his Latin grammar.

"You like to study, my son?" asked the plump little priest.

Louis's face kindled. "Oh, yes, Monseigneur," he said eagerly. "I love books."

The bishop nodded, well pleased. When Louis was a little older, Taché gave him free run of the library, and Louis spent hours poring over heavy tomes of literature and philosophy. The bishop began to think that this clever, pious youngster might be just who he was looking for – someone who might someday become the first Métis priest in the North-West.

And so, in June of 1858, thirteen-year-old Louis found himself standing in the sunshine on the steps outside St. Boniface Cathedral. He had just heard mass with his family, and his soul was still aglow with the mystery and wonder of it. Sara, her eyes wide and shining in her thin face, tugged on his sleeve.

"How proud you must be, Louis! And we are all so proud of you," she said. But even as she spoke, tears welled up in her eyes.

Louis couldn't speak for the lump in his own throat. He was proud to be one of three boys chosen to study at a college in Montreal. But it was so far away! He couldn't even imagine such a journey. He would have to live in a great city, shut away from the fields and woods he loved. And he would not to be able to see his family again – for years! Swallowing hard, he hugged his mother and gave her a loving message for his father, who was away on a business trip. Then there were all his brothers and sisters to hug, and Sara, the last of all.

"I'm afraid I won't be able to bear it, Sara," he whispered. "Unless God helps me."

"He will, Louis. I know He will!" Sara gazed up at him with adoring eyes, sure that when she saw her beloved brother again he would be all grown up. A man. A priest.

2

Into the World

They journeyed across a prairie bursting into summer bloom. Beside the rutted wagon track, cow
parsley and wild indigo nodded in the springy new
grass. Perched atop a jolting cart, Louis peered eagerly
ahead through clouds of dust. This was his first trip
away from home – his first trip anywhere. At the end of
the long, hot day, they camped for the night, and he
and his companions went exploring. Later, rolled in
their blankets, they talked among themselves before
drifting off to sleep under the stars.

"I hope we see some Sioux!" whispered Louis.

"Not me!" said Louis Schmidt. "They're fierce!"

Daniel McDougall shivered. "I want to go home,"
he whimpered.

Riel at the age of 22. He was a law clerk,
and he was courting Marie-Julie Guernon.

"I'll look after you," Louis promised.

As they approached Red Lake, Louis glimpsed a familiar figure. "Papa!" he yelled, scrambling down from the cart.

"Louis, my boy!" Jean-Louis Riel caught him up in a fierce bear hug.

"You've been away a whole year, Papa! And now I'm going away to school."

They had only a few minutes together before the tripmen wanted to leave. Louis knelt for his father's blessing. "Study hard, my son. I'll be proud to see you come back to us a priest," Jean-Louis told him.

Louis looked back until the beloved figure was no more than a dot on the shore of the lake.

After twenty-eight days, the travellers reached St. Paul, on the Mississippi. Louis and the other boys gawked at the mighty river and the bustling frontier town. The next day they headed downstream on a steamboat, its great paddlewheel thrashing the muddy water. At Prairie du Chien, another wonder awaited them – a steam train. Huffing and puffing, cinders flying, a succession of trains whirled the boys past a blur of cities – Chicago, Detroit, Hamilton, Toronto. At last, on the evening of July 5, they arrived in Montreal. Their journey had lasted five weeks and covered 2400 kilometres. At the convent of the Grey Nuns, Sister Valade, their escort, handed them over to the Mother Superior. "The farther they journeyed," she sighed, "the more unruly they became!"

The next morning, Louis woke up early. Peering out a narrow window, he saw a sea of roofs. And the steeples – never had he seen so many churches!

"When will we go to our school?" he asked the Mother Superior after breakfast.

"Ah, but you are not all going to the same school," she replied. "You, Louis Riel, will go to the Collège de Montréal. But Louis Schmidt and Daniel McDougall will go to different schools outside the city."

"But we want to be together!" protested Louis.

"We all must obey God's will," she reminded him.

Louis's heart sank at the sight of the gloomy Collège de Montréal. It was surrounded by a high wall, and when the iron gate clanged shut behind him he flinched like a prairie fox caught in a trap. At first he ached with homesickness, his high spirits quenched. But he soon found out that the strict routine of the school left him little time to brood. Every day, he and the other students rose early and ate a breakfast of barley porridge. After that came mass, and after that, morning classes. Lunch was a bite of bread and cheese, and then there were more classes. There were no organized sports. Dinner was always the same – boiled beef, plain and grey. As he chewed the beef, Louis listened with the rest to a boy reading dull passages from an "improving" book. Then he studied, said his prayers, and went to bed. He was not allowed to leave the college during the school year or even read a newspaper. The boys' Saturday treat was a bath, and they did their own laundry. Louis hated that.

He entered the second year of an eight-year course. He studied Greek and Latin, French literature, English, philosophy, and mathematics. At first Louis's grades were not high, but soon his marks improved. By the end of October 1858, he stood thirteenth in a class of thirty-seven, though he was competing against boys from the best schools of French Canada.

Right from the start, Louis knew how to make himself popular. At recess, other boys gathered around eagerly to hear his Wild West stories.

"*Bien sûr*, I've seen Sioux," he told them. "They have long hair, and you should see their tomahawks. Why, I was nearly scalped once."

His listeners' mouths dropped open.

"*Mais, oui!* And once I was almost burnt up in a prairie fire. And a friend of mine was trampled by a wild horse. And speaking of horses, why, I once saw a hunter jump his horse right across a river, chasing a buffalo!"

He became fiercely loyal to his new friends. When one boy caught smallpox and lay dying, Louis prayed by the boy's bedside, refusing to leave. He also became known for his high standards. If he caught anyone cheating during a game, he would stalk away without a word. But most of all, Louis hated any kind of bullying.

"Have you met Quinn yet?" a friend asked him one day. "He's Irish, you know. Just off the boat. That's him over there."

Louis saw a knot of boys gathered under the poplars of the recreation ground. At their centre, a gangling lad turned helplessly from one tormentor to another.

"What's wrong with your arms, Quinn? They look stuck on, like handles on a basket!"

"And he hasn't got his land legs yet. Just look at that rolling gait!" There was jeering laughter as Quinn broke through the crowd and tried to get away.

In a few bounds, Louis reached him. "Leave him alone! The poor fellow hasn't done anything to you!" he cried. "Anyway, if England had made you eat as many potatoes as he has had to eat, you wouldn't be any more solid on your legs than poor Quinn!"

Putting his arm about the new boy's shoulders, Louis walked off with him. From then on, he became Quinn's best and only friend.

∞

Louis spent his first summer vacations with Louis Schmidt and Daniel McDougall. Sometimes they stayed at the home of Bishop Taché's family, sometimes with Madame Marie-Geneviève-Sophie Masson, the benefactress who had paid to bring them to study in the East. The Grey Nuns also invited the boys to their residence on the St. Lawrence River. There they were taken out in a boat to run the rapids at Sault St. Louis.

"Hang on tight!" warned the boatman, and Louis Schmidt and Daniel clung fearfully to the side of the boat.

But Louis, thrilled, leaned over the bow as the boat shot through the whitewater. "It's glorious!" he cried.

By the summer of 1861, though, the other boys had returned to Red River, because Louis Schimdt's health had failed and Daniel McDougall was incurably homesick. Only Louis remained to fulfill Bishop Taché's hopes. When the school term ended, he still spent part of each summer with the Massons, where he associated with wealthy, polished people. He and Madame Masson's son Rodrigue became fast friends.

"Now you're about in the world, we must smarten you up a bit," the young lawyer said, looking him up and down.

"You'll never make a dandy out of me," warned Louis.

But he drank in Rodrigue's advice and learned how to dress and what to say in a drawing room. He blotted up French-Canadian history and culture, too. The Massons were enthusiastic about politics, and Louis picked up some of their ideas. The family supported the Parti bleu, which had a policy of French-Canadian nationalism and moderate reform. Their great leader was George-Étienne Cartier. *Les bleus* believed that the best way to guard French-Canadian values was through the supremacy of the Church over the State. This made sense to Louis, steeped as he was in religion.

He spent the rest of his summer vacations with his aunt, Lucie Lee, and her husband, who had a comfortable stone house in Mile End, on the outskirts of Montreal. The next-door neighbours, it turned out, had a daughter about Louis's age.

"Who's that pretty girl?" he asked, after seeing her in church.

"Oh, that's Marie-Julie Guernon," replied his aunt.

About this time, Louis began to write poetry. He wrote many fables in verse, in which good was rewarded and evil punished. The best, "The Cat and the Mice," tells of a cruel cat – "very English by birth" – that preys for years upon a group of mice. At last they rebel. Though many of them are killed in the attempt, they attack the cat and blind it.

> To the mice went the victory,
> With losses, yet with glory.
> At last they could taste
> The joy of revenge. And beneath their little roofs
> Their descendants would long recall it.
> As for our sly puss,
> He suffered and died mad.
> Thus is righteousness avenged.

Clearly, Louis was on the side of the French-Canadian "mice." He also remembered his father's defiance of the Hudson's Bay Company.

∞

By 1863, Louis had grown into a broad-shouldered young man with high cheekbones and deep-set, piercing eyes. He was still very popular, though his friends joked that his fiery pride would never allow him to admit he could be wrong – about anything. Then, early in 1864, Louis learned that his father had died. Shaken to the core, he wept bitterly and poured out his suffering in prayers. On February 23, he wrote to his family:

> Let us weep, but let our hearts be strong; let us think of God: he loves us for He has terribly afflicted us... You know dear mother, brothers, and sisters, when God acts it is

always with generosity. Let us adore him
then! May he be blessed, glorified!... Love
the hand of God; whatever it does it is always
paternal.

Louis remained depressed, but somehow pulled himself together and did well in his March examinations.
But he was nervous, and often rebelled against his
teachers. Should I really become a priest? he wondered. After all, I'm head of the family now. How can I
look after my brothers and sisters if I'm a priest?

Then, at Mile End that summer, Louis's emotions
underwent another upheaval. He suddenly began
entering love poems in his poetry book. They are
undated, but the first is entered after another poem
dated July 3, 1864. In it, a dying lover begs his love to
remember him, and to visit his grave. In a second
poem, the poet says "Marie" rejects him because love is
fickle, and also because her mother disapproves. Yet he
still believes he has won her heart. But in the third
poem, the mother cruelly tells the young lover,

> My daughter's too gentle
> To marry a bandit.
> She is far too refined
> For you, without doubt.
>
> She is far too refined
> For you, without doubt.
> So for my Cécile
> You may count yourself out.

Louis had fallen head over heels in love with Marie-Julie Guernon. But Marie-Julie's family had discovered the romance, and Madame Guernon was not pleased. It's not clear why, for Louis was handsome and well educated, and his relatives were prosperous neighbours. Was Madame Guernon scandalized because Louis was studying to be a priest? Or did she disapprove because he was a Métis? The word "bandit" in the third poem may be a clue.

The young couple went on seeing one another, though, for in a fourth poem, Louis says, "love is the secret of happiness." Sometime during the autumn of 1864, he chose love and family duty over the priesthood, and in December 1864, he visited Madame Masson's agent.

"I want to enter a profession," Louis told him. "Or get a job in a store."

The agent's eyebrows shot up. "Aren't you going to be a priest?" he asked.

Louis shook his head. "My tastes lead me into the world," he said. "And I hope to help settle my young brothers and sisters."

Nothing came of the interview. There were only a few months to go before Louis would get his degree, but he neglected his schoolwork and rebelled against college discipline. In February he went to board with the Grey Nuns. There he broke curfew and even stayed out all night. He said he was looking for work, and stayed away from classes for fifteen days. Fed up, the Director expelled him from the Collège on March 8, and Louis went to stay with the Lees in Mile End.

"I've made my choice," he told Marie-Julie, putting a brave face on it. "I'll soon get a job, and then we'll be married."

Marie-Julie's face glowed under her fur cap. "I hope it will be soon, Louis," she whispered.

He first thought of going into the fur trade, and even boasted to a friend of Bishop Taché's that a backer had promised him £1000 as capital. But perhaps the money was only wishful thinking, for Louis lingered in Montreal. He didn't write home, and his friends and family fretted about him. In January 1866, he began writing to George-Étienne Cartier, the leader of the Parti bleu. Cartier was an old boy of the Collège de Montréal, and Louis hoped the eminent politician might help him. He wrote two letters to Cartier, then sent him a long verse, which began:

> In the midst of the crowd
> So uneasy and restless,
> There appears a man with a thoughtful brow;
> At his air of nobility
> And expression of sadness
> People cast furtive glances.
> If he speaks, they will whisper
> Brothers, who is this fellow then?
> But the only attention he arouses
> Is a vague concern.
> Under gloomy skies, he goes on
> Lost in cares,
> His heart filled with sighs.
> His life long and hard;
> For it is empty of joy!

But still Cartier did not reply. Then, just when all seemed lost, Riel found a position in the office of Rodolphe Laflamme, a well-known lawyer who supported the Parti rouge. *Les rouges* were liberal and believed the Church should stay out of politics. They thought that French-Canadian language and culture might be best protected in a republic.

"Now, none of your *bleu* ideas will do here, mind," Laflamme warned, wagging a finger at Louis.

"No, sir," said Louis. Laflamme's liberal politics felt like a plunge into hot water, but he was desperate for work.

He couldn't wait to tell Marie-Julie the good news.

"I'm going to be a lawyer," he said proudly. "Your parents can't object now!"

On June 12, 1866, Louis and Marie-Julie signed a wedding contract without the knowledge of her parents. Louis agreed not to request a dowry, and to a strict separation of property. But when the forthcoming marriage was announced in the church at Mile End the following Sunday, Marie-Julie's parents were outraged.

"You have no business trying to marry my daughter!" stormed Madame Guernon. "And you, Julie, what were you thinking of?"

"But Maman, Louis has a job now. He…"

"*Silence!*"

"Don't you care for Marie-Julie's happiness?" protested Louis.

Madame Guernon rounded on him. "Too much to allow her to marry the likes of you!" she snapped.

Before long, Louis received a note that broke his heart. Marie-Julie wrote that she could not disobey her parents. She was breaking their engagement.

Just days later, on June 19, 1866, Louis left Montreal. He had failed in his "mission" to be the first Métis priest in the West. Now he was giving up the law too. He did have a good education to show for his seven years of hard work, but he felt deep guilt for having abandoned his vocation. And his failed romance scorched his pride. Somewhere, somehow, I will prove myself, he vowed.

A farm in the Red River Settlement. By 1869, Métis had been farming in this area for generations.

St. Boniface Cathedral. Louis Riel attended mass here. In 1860 the cathedral burned down, but when Riel returned to Red River in 1868 it had been rebuilt. From the steps of the cathedral, in 1869 he warned of the danger to Métis interests when Canada took over the colony.

3

Who Will Lead Our People?

On a beautiful summer morning in 1868, Riel leaned against the railing of a steamboat thrashing its way down the Red River. Around a bend, St. Boniface Cathedral appeared against the blue vault of the prairie sky, and tears sprang to Louis's eyes. The church was new to him, for the old one with its twin spires had burned down in 1860. But on that spot he had been blessed and sent out into the world with so many hopes. And now he was back, with none of them fulfilled. He turned his gaze to the convent of the Grey Nuns. Was Sara looking out of one of the windows? For in 1861 she had entered the convent as a novice.

Now he could see for himself how much Red River had changed. North of Fort Garry, a new village called Winnipeg had sprung up. Nearly fifteen thousand people lived in the Red River Settlement now, and, along with the rest of Rupert's Land, it would soon become part of the new Dominion of Canada. This much he knew from his talks with Métis traders south of the border.

Two years had passed since Louis left Montreal. His account of his doings in these years is terse: "Left Montreal 19th June, 1866. Came to St. Paul, lived in Minneapolis, St. Anthony and Saint Paul 2 years. Left St. Anthony in July 68 and came to St. Joe, Dakota." All the while, he had worried about money. By the summer of 1867, he was in St. Paul. From there, he wrote to his mother, "You are always in my thoughts. You know how much I love you, my good mother and my little brothers and sisters. I am sad that I cannot make you as happy as you would like."

Everywhere he went, Riel sought out fellow francophones, like the French-Canadian settlers who lived in St. Anthony, north of Minneapolis. Riel felt at home there, and he could gossip about Red River with Métis freighters, too. He held various jobs, one of them in a dry goods store. Then, in 1868, he was sent by a St. Paul merchant on business to the Métis village of St. Joseph, near the border. From there it was only a brief trip home.

But even home was not the same.

"So you left the old place," Louis said to his mother, looking around the new homestead. It was in the parish of St. Vital, on the east bank of the Red River. The house was built of logs and had two storeys, a big stone fireplace, and a kitchen wing.

Julie Riel smiled. "Yes, my son. The land is better for farming here. And we're closer to my family."

"Now your Lagimodière tongues can wag to your hearts' content," he teased.

"And Henriette and I can walk to school now," piped up Alexandre, the "baby" of the family. He and Henriette had been born since Louis left Red River, and Alexandre had attached himself like a limpet to his grand brother.

Louis's mother gazed at him fondly. Her darling had come back, when they most needed him. And how could she not be proud of such a splendid-looking fellow, who spoke so beautifully and looked such a gentleman?

"Now, tell me everything," said Louis, sitting down at the kitchen table.

"It's been two terrible years," blurted Charles. "First the grasshoppers ate everything. Then the buffalo disappeared, so the hunters have no money. People are starving!"

Louis nodded, and squeezed his arm. For he knew Charles had had to leave school to work in his uncle's mill and help bring in a little money.

"And not just the buffalo," added Joseph. "There's not a fish in the lake or a rabbit on the prairie!"

"And a tornado hit the Anglican church in Winnipeg!" put in Octavie, eager to tell the best bit.

Louis pulled a long face. "*Vraiment?* And what did the Anglicans do to deserve it?" he asked.

"We did get a small harvest last year," said Charles, when the laughter died down. "And we still have the livestock."

"And Charles shares what he earns," said Julie Riel proudly. "And Marie, too."

Sara, Louis learned, was teaching at the Grey Nuns' mission at St. Norbert. He soon rode over to visit her. He was shocked to see Sara in her sober grey habit, her face framed by a stiff white coif. The love for him in her eyes was the same, yet an unspoken "but" lingered between them. He knew she still hoped he would become a priest.

Riel also visited the parish priest, Father Noël-Joseph Ritchot.

"I think you will be a man like your father," the priest told him. "One who cares about his people."

"Every day I hope to follow in his footsteps," Louis said eagerly. He soon made a habit of talking with Father Ritchot about the situation in Red River. The priest listened gravely, stroking his flowing black beard, and asking a keen question now and then.

At harvest time, Riel set to work on the farm. He had not done heavy labour for a long time. His muscles ached and his soft gentleman's hands blistered and cracked. The harvest that year was meagre. They salvaged some grain and potatoes from their drought-stricken fields, but Louis knew they would have to accept seed grain for next year's crop from the famine relief committee.

Though Riel stuck to his labours, he sometimes wondered how long he could keep it up. He loved his family dearly, yet life at the Riel homestead was a bit suffocating. After all, he was a grown man. He had lived in a wider world. His time had been his own and he had had his privacy. Now he shared sleeping quarters with his young brothers. And wherever he went about the farm, indoors or out, his family's faces followed him, like sunflowers seeking the sun. So much depended on him. Yet he knew in his heart that Red River was a dead end for him. There were simply no jobs for a Métis with a fancy education.

Longing for someone his own age to talk to, he asked Louis Schmidt to come for a long visit. But when his old friend showed up on the doorstep, Riel sized up his hangdog appearance in a glance. Schmidt had managed to get nothing but a series of small hand-to-mouth jobs. Louis felt a chill around his heart. Might this be his future too, if he remained in Red River?

Night after night, once the family was abed, Riel and Schmidt discussed the kind of place Red River had become. It didn't make for pleasant hearing.

"Protestants and Catholics have always disagreed, surely?" Louis asked. "And the whites with the mixed-bloods, too. About all people agreed on is that they hated the Hudson's Bay Company."

"They still do," said Schmidt. "But now they hate each other too. Thanks to the meddling of bigoted clergymen, the Protestants think we Catholics are agents of the devil. Even the mixed-bloods think the same. Our Indian heritage isn't enough to paper over the cracks."

"And the so-called Canadian party?" Louis asked.

"A bunch of carpetbaggers from Ontario out to make fast fortunes by buying land low, hoping to sell it high if Canada takes over," snorted Schmidt. "Bigoted, too. Anyone with Indian blood is dust beneath their boots."

"I hear Schultz is their leader."

Schmidt nodded. A red-haired giant of a man, Dr. John Schultz had established a general store in Winnipeg. He despised the First Nations people, mixed-bloods, and Métis of Red River, and gathered like-minded people around him.

One night, Riel and Schmidt talked almost until morning, Louis pacing back and forth before the dying fire. "If Canada takes over, our culture and our faith will be drowned in a flood of English-speaking Protestants from Ontario," he said at last. "Is there no one to lead our people?"

Schmidt shook his head. "No," he said. "Though not all of us are helpless. The big merchants do well and live comfortably. They have contracts with the Company. Some of them – Monsieur Breland, Monsieur Goulet – sit on the Council of Assiniboia. But the last thing they want is to stir up trouble, though they know they will suffer if Canada takes over. That will mean high trade tariffs and railroads. The end of freighting by ox cart."

Riel stroked his glossy moustache. "But what will happen to the little people? The boatmen? The hunters?"

"Doomed," said Schmidt. "The West is changing. The buffalo are going – you know there were none this year. No buffalo means no meat or buffalo robes, and that means no money for supplies. To make matters worse, the fashion has changed in Europe, people say. Silk hats are in, beaver hats are out. That will harm the fur trade."

A smouldering log rolled out of the hearth, and Riel kicked it back, sending a shower of sparks volleying up the chimney. "We Métis can't just sit like ptarmigan waiting to be shot!" he protested. "We must act!"

"But what can we do?"

"We'll know when the time comes," said Louis.

They shook hands on it.

In November, Louis heard that the writer Charles Mair had arrived to join the Canadian party. In January, a letter of Mair's containing an account of Red River was published in the Toronto *Globe*. It painted a rosy picture of the colony's prospects.

"No mention of floods, drought, early frosts, or plagues of grasshoppers," Riel complained to Schmidt. "And he said the only reason that 'half-breeds' were starving was because they wouldn't farm!"

"He insulted the mixed-blood ladies, too. Said they lack a pedigree, and backbite the white ladies," said Schmidt.

In Winnipeg, Mrs. Annie Bannatyne, the mixed-blood wife of a prosperous merchant, decided to avenge this insult. She found out when Mair picked up his mail; then, armed with a riding whip, she sashayed down to the general store. When Mair showed up, she pulled his nose and walloped him with the riding crop. "There," she said. "You see how the women of Red River treat those who insult them!"

All Red River rocked with laughter. Riel sat down and wrote a gleeful ditty, which people began to sing. It goes in part,

Let's set ourselves to wring
La-i-tou-trà-là

Let's set ourselves to wring
The nose of this dogfish
   Down there!
It's a lady who shows us
La-i-tou-trà-là
It's a lady who shows us
How we must treat them
   Down there!

And he did more. Not long afterward, on February 25, the following letter appeared in *Le Nouveau Monde*, a Montreal newspaper:

Red River. February 1, 1869
Mr. Editor:
Please be so good as to give me a little space in the columns of your journal, so that I too may write of Red River. I cannot resist that temptation since I have read the outrages which a journal of Upper Canada has just uttered in publishing a letter of a certain Mr. Mair, who arrived in Red River last fall... Only a month after his arrival in this country, Mr. Mair set out to describe it and its inhabitants.

The writer of the letter then pointed out that Mair had not told the truth about Red River and its people. And he rejected Mair's claim that only "half-breeds" had accepted help from the famine relief committee.

I am a half-breed myself and I say that there is nothing falser than those words. I know almost all the names of those who received help this winter, and I can assure you that they were of all colours. There are some half-breeds who do not ask for charity, as there are some English, some Germans and some Scots who receive it every week...

The letter was signed L.R.

Part Two

Blaze

Louis Riel, the fiery young leader of his people.

4

Loyal Subject of Her Majesty

By late June, the fields of the Riel farm were hazed with the tender green of new grain. At least the seed from the famine relief committee meant they had a crop, Riel told himself as he gazed out over the family land. Now if only the rains would arrive – and the grasshoppers would not!

He stretched, enjoying the warmth of the sun on his back. Nearly a year had passed since his return to Red River, and his work as a farmer showed. His skin was deeply tanned, and he had filled out. His city suit felt uncomfortably tight in the shoulders now, though he had few chances to wear it. And he did not expect to see a city any time soon. In March he had written to a merchant he knew in St. Paul, hoping for a job. But he had had no reply.

Even Louis Schmidt was doing better than he. "I've been paid a bit of money I was owed," he told Louis. "I've bought some oxen and Red River carts. I'm going to freight goods to St. Paul. Why don't you join me – come in as my partner?"

"Why not?" Louis had said. It would bring in some money, and be a change from farming. But in the end, he didn't go. Something held him in Red River.

What he wanted, he knew, was to help his people as he and Schmidt had planned. The Hudson's Bay Company was rumoured to have sold Rupert's Land to the Dominion of Canada for £300,000. Now the Canadian government would appoint a lieutenant-governor and council to deal with its new territory. The people of Red River grumbled that they had been sold like a flock of sheep. But Louis was impatient with talk. He felt in his bones that the Métis must do something. But what?

∞

Then events began to move. In late June, Charles Mair and John Snow, an Ontarian in charge of building a road to Canada, began pacing out lots on Métis land. Caught with a bundle of survey stakes, they were driven off the land by angry Métis. Louis was pleased when he heard of it. It was more than good, he told himself. It was hopeful. If the Canadians kept pushing, the Métis were bound to resist. And then...

On July 5, a meeting of Métis was called. In times of danger, it was their custom to elect captains to lead them. That day they chose two senior Métis to arrange patrols of the neighbourhood and keep strangers off

Métis land. They did this just in time, for news soon arrived that English settlers had dug a well and were felling trees in one of the Métis parishes.

The Métis were now seriously worried. On July 29, a man named William Dease called a meeting of Métis and First Nations people at the courthouse. He gave a fiery speech, suggesting that the £300,000 to be paid by Canada to the Hudson's Bay Company belonged by right to them.

"And," he said, "why not take over the property of the Company in Red River by force until they pay us?"

An uneasy silence fell on the crowd. Then a Métis elder named John Bruce stood up to speak. "No, brothers," he said. "That is not the right way to proceed."

There was a storm of applause, and Riel, who was sitting nearby, sprang to his feet. "I support Monsieur Bruce," he said, glancing around. Around him, heads nodded, approving his respect for the older man. They know whose son I am, Louis told himself as he sat down, and that I'm the best-educated Métis in Red River. Let them ponder that!

∞

On a Sunday morning near the end of August, Riel stood on the steps of St. Boniface Cathedral. Around him was a crowd of worshippers who had just attended mass.

"Beware," he told them. "Surveyors have arrived from Canada to steal your land."

The crowd stirred uneasily. Everybody had heard about the survey party.

"They say," Louis went on, "they say that Métis land holdings are not in danger." His tone gave the words a scornful twist. "If that is so, why does not the government of Canada send us guarantees?"

There was a mutter of agreement, for this was a sore point. Months had passed, and the Canadian government had not sent any guarantees that the lands of the Red River settlers would be respected after the takeover.

"Colonel Dennis is their leader," Riel said, smiling now. "Who knows? He may be a splendid fellow. He certainly has splendid mutton-chop whiskers!"

Laughter swept the crowd.

Riel held up his hand. "But this same Colonel Dennis – where is he staying? With John Schultz, our sworn enemy! How can we trust such a man?" People nodded, and Louis knew he had them in the palm of his hand. "Let us wait, let us watch. But *en garde, en garde!*" he concluded.

Soon afterwards, the surveyors set to work near Métis land at Oak Point, and Louis chuckled when he heard that the Métis had sent them packing. Colonel Dennis then shifted the survey, and his men began working their way north from near the American border. But tensions simmered, as more and more English-speaking settlers arrived. And still the Canadian government sent no guarantees that existing land holdings would be honoured.

"Have you heard about our new lieutenant-governor?" Riel asked Father Ritchot. "He's none other than the Honourable William McDougall. The former Canadian Minister of Public Works."

Father Ritchot stroked his beard. "Ah. The very man who sent us Messieurs Mair, Snow, and Dennis," he said mildly.

"The three plagues!" Louis snorted. "And he has already appointed three members to the new governing council – men of whom we know nothing!"

Riel was working hard to build up his influence among the Métis. He visited people on their farms and chatted on the road or over a fence at harvest time. His message was always the same. The Canadians were not to be trusted. The Métis must unite to protect their rights. Patrols were not enough – they needed a Métis central committee to keep an eye on things. During September, the Métis held secret meetings in Father Ritchot's presbytery in St. Norbert. Two men were elected from each Métis parish to form a committee, and Riel acted as secretary.

The surveys were getting close to Red River again, so on October 1, Riel went to see Colonel Dennis. He squeezed into his city suit, but on his feet he wore moccasins. He liked to feel the ground under his feet.

"I have some little education," Riel began modestly. "So my brethren have asked me to inquire what is being done with the country. They are in a state of great excitement about the surveys."

Dennis stroked his magnificent whiskers. "But my dear fellow," he blustered, "our survey will not affect Métis land at all! Why, the Canadian government plans to grant free titles to all existing landholders. And of course it will pay to extinguish Indian claims on the land as well."

Riel raised his eyebrows. "I'm delighted to hear that the government's intentions are so just and so liberal," he said. "I will certainly make this known among my people."

The Colonel bowed him out, pleased to have poured oil on troubled waters.

But Riel was not convinced. On October 6 he penned a letter to *Le Courrier de Saint-Hyacinthe*, a Quebec newspaper edited by an old college friend of his. The Métis of Red River, he assured the readers, were loyal subjects of the Queen. So they had the same rights as settlers in other British colonies. But their rights were being endangered by a survey conducted by an alien power – Canada – without their consent. Louis hoped this letter would spark sympathy in Quebec for the Métis cause.

On October 11, 1869, Dennis's survey team had completed its work south of Red River. It went on to survey a baseline near the settlement. And that line ran right through the "hay privilege" of Édouard Marion. The hay privilege was the rear half of each narrow riverfront farm that was left in prairie grass and used as common grazing land. It was to defend this land right that Riel and the other Métis set their feet upon the survey chain and forced the surveyors to retreat.

"Don't they know about the hay privilege?" one Métis asked as the survey wagons rolled away.

"They know now!" said Louis.

The next day, Riel was sent for by William Mactavish, who governed the settlement for the Hudson's Bay Company. The Governor had warned Dennis that the survey would cause problems. Deathly ill with tuberculosis, Mactavish did not want trouble.

"Dennis tells me you and some others stopped his survey crew yesterday. Why?" the shrewd old Scotsman demanded.

Riel's eyes flashed. "The Canadian government has no right to make surveys on the territory without the express permission of the people of the settlement," he replied. That was his opinion, and he stuck to it.

∞

The confrontation boosted Riel's popularity among the Métis. And now he had new sources of support. Métis voyageurs had returned to the settlement for the winter from the far West. The Métis who manned the Company boats between Fort Garry and York Factory and the Saskatchewan were back too. Louis knew these men were daredevils, ready for anything. They would be the muscle behind his resistance movement. He could now act, despite the doubts of cautious Métis who feared confronting the Canadian government.

On October 16, Riel called a mass meeting at St. Norbert. Delegates were elected to a new organization called the National Committee. John Bruce was elected president, and Louis once more became secretary. The Committee quickly passed a resolution to create a military force with captains and soldiers. Within days, four hundred men had been recruited. Many were armed with muskets, revolvers, or hunting knives.

Riel knew that the new lieutenant-governor was on his way to Red River by way of the United States.

The latest rumour said he was bringing three hundred rifles with him. So, on October 17, the National Committee sent forty horsemen to barricade the only road that led to Red River from the south, at a point where it crossed the Rivière Sale. The three-foot-high roadblock was built of fence timber, with a gate in the middle. Two sentries armed with muskets stood on duty on either side of it. The rest of the horsemen camped nearby. On October 21, the Committee sent the following letter to await McDougall at Pembina, just south of the border:

> Sir,
> The National Committee of the Métis of Red River orders William McDougall not to enter the Territory of the North-West without special permission of the above-mentioned committee.
>
> By the order of the President, John Bruce.
> Louis Riel, Secretary.

Again, Riel addressed the Sunday crowd outside the cathedral.

"Would it be easier to let McDougall into Red River?" he demanded. "Yes! But then we will lose our political rights."

His eyes searched their faces. "We must stop him!" he cried, his excitement kindling. "And if a Métis should be killed in the conflict, we will dip a handkerchief in his blood and make it our national flag!"

There were cheers, but some people shook their heads. Young Riel sounded as radical as his father.

On October 25, Riel and Bruce were summoned before the Council of Assiniboia, the governing body of Red River.

"Your roadblock is illegal," the head of the council told them. You must take it down."

Louis was defiant. "We will not!" he shot back. "We Métis object to any government coming from Canada without our being consulted in the matter."

"But why?"

"Why?" echoed Riel. "Because many of my people are uneducated and only half civilized. They fear that if a large immigration takes place they will be crowded out of a country which they claim as their own!"

There were angry protests from members of the council.

"No, no, that's wrong!"

"If you keep McDougall out the consequences may be disastrous for all of us!"

Louis held his ground, scowling. "Well," he conceded at last, "I will tell my supporters what you have said. That is all."

Riel knew very well that the council had no military force to back up its decisions. And if it called out volunteers to stop the Métis there would be civil war in Red River. He was gambling that this would not happen. In the end, the council sent a message to Pembina warning McDougall that for his own good he should not cross the border.

Governor Mactavish made one last effort. He sent for Riel on October 28. Too ill to get out of bed, he lay struggling to breathe, his face as white as his pillows.

"Your father was a man who knew how to serve this settlement," he began.

"I, too, hope to serve my country," Louis replied proudly.

"Then why not give the Canadian government a chance, lad?" pleaded Mactavish.

Louis shook his head. "It is only prudence to prevent the wolf's entry into the sheep-pen. It looks to us as if it would be easier to keep the wolf outside in the first place than to have to throw it out later."

"What is this talk of wolves?" Mactavish demanded.

"To us the Canadian Government *is a wolf,*" retorted Riel. "We are determined to prevent its entry into our country, where it has no right. We remain loyal subjects of Her Majesty, but we refuse point-blank to recognize the authority of Canada until after it treats with us!"

5

Resistance

On the morning of November 2, 1869, Riel led a band of Métis through the woods along the Red and Assiniboine rivers. Keeping under cover, they headed toward Upper Fort Garry. Riel entered and asked to speak to William Cowan, who was in charge. While the two men talked, 120 armed Métis, in small groups, slipped inside the unwatched gates of the fort.

When he learned what had happened, Cowan rounded on Riel. "What are these men doing here?" he demanded.

"They have come to guard the fort," said Riel, politely.

"Guard it? Against whom?" spluttered Cowan.

Upper Fort Garry, the main western base of the Hudson's Bay Company fur trade. Riel made it the nerve centre of the Red River Resistance in 1869-70.

"Against a danger which I have reason to believe threatens it," replied Riel. He promised that his men would not bother anyone or disturb private property.

Riel had seized the strategic centre of Red River, with its fortified walls and cannons. All the roads and river routes in the North-West ended at Upper Fort Garry. Now Métis patrols could control traffic in and out of the settlement and confiscate any firearms they found. And Fort Garry contained valuable supplies Louis needed to maintain his troops.

Meanwhile, Ambroise Lépine, Riel's second-in-command, was carrying out the rest of his plan. Lieutenant-Governor McDougall had arrived in Pembina on October 30. He crossed into Canada and stopped at the Hudson's Bay Company post just north of the border. While Riel occupied Fort Garry, armed Métis horsemen rode down to confront McDougall.

"You must return to Pembina tomorrow, sir," Lépine told him. They escorted the furious man back to the United States the next morning. But his luggage wagons, which had gone ahead to the barricade, they took to Red River.

"Our would-be ruler is back across the border," Lépine reported to Riel. "But we brought you his throne." Amid guffaws of laughter, a grinning Métis held up McDougall's fancy toilet seat.

∞

Riel knew he had to win the support of the English-speaking people of Red River. If they declared themselves against him, it would mean civil war, and the

Canadian government would refuse to negotiate. So, on November 6, he invited the English-speakers to send twelve representatives to meet with twelve French-speaking delegates. They would "consider the present political state of this Country, and adopt such measures as may be deemed best for the future welfare of the same."

Louis knew the anglophones disapproved of him, but he was offering them a chance to have their say. On November 16, their delegates arrived at the Red River courthouse. Cannons boomed from the turrets of the fort, and the crackle of a *feu de joie* echoed off its stone walls.

"An enthusiastic welcome, gentlemen," said Louis, bowing.

But the anglophones scowled at the Métis' display of their military strength, and the meetings were prickly. The main problem was McDougall. The English-speaking delegates wanted him admitted to the settlement, but Riel refused. Then Governor Mactavish issued a proclamation listing the "unlawful acts" of Riel and his men. He said they must evacuate the fort and allow McDougall into the settlement. For, he said, "You are dealing with a crisis out of which may come incalculable good or immeasurable evil."

James Ross, the main speaker for the anglophones, turned to Riel in triumph. "You and your men are rebels, sir," he cried. "You must disband at once!"

Louis leapt to his feet. "If we are rebels," he shot back, "we are rebels against the Company that sold us, and is ready to hand us over, and against Canada that wants to buy us. We are not in rebellion against the British supremacy which has still not given its approval for the final transfer of the country." Glancing around the room, he could see heads nodding. Softening his tone, he went on, "Moreover, we are true to our native land. We are protecting it against the dangers that threaten it. We want the people of Red River to be a free people. Let us help one another. We are all brothers and relations, says Mr. Ross, and it is true. Let us not separate. See what Mr. Mactavish says. He says that out of this meeting and its decision may come incalculable good. Let us unite. The evil that he fears will not take place. See how he speaks. Is it surprising? His children are half-breeds like ourselves."

He had played the best card he had, the common aboriginal heritage of the Métis and the English-speaking mixed-bloods. In the end, all the delegates stayed. But the council could not agree about McDougall.

∞

Riel soon acted again. On November 23, he took over the land registers and accounts of the Council of Assiniboia. And later the same day, he tried to push matters even further.

"The Council of Assiniboia is dead," he told the assembled delegates. "We must form a provisional government to run the settlement and negotiate with Canada."

There was a shocked murmur, and men stared at each other. Even some of the Métis looked worried.

"You are going too far!" Ross warned Riel. "The Canadian government will send a military expedition if we do not adopt a moderate position."

"Winter protects us," Louis replied coolly. "No route to Red River is open in winter. We have six months to get a favourable settlement out of them."

While the council dithered, Louis fretted about the Canadian party. He knew they were in touch with McDougall in Pembina. Canada was supposed to assume responsibility for Red River and the rest of the North-West on December 1, and the Canadians urged McDougall to issue this proclamation on schedule. So on that day, McDougall trudged across the border and read his proclamation into a howling blizzard. Then he scurried back to Pembina.

At the next council meeting, Ross got to his feet. "As we all knew, the lieutenant-governor has issued his proclamation," he said.

"What does that matter?" said Riel. "We Métis won't let him into Red River until our rights are secure. If he guarantees our rights, why, I am one of those who will go to meet him and escort him here."

"What rights shall we ask him to guarantee?" demanded Ross.

So Riel and the Métis drew up a List of Rights. They wanted people to elect their own legislature, which would have to approve all laws concerning them passed by the Parliament of Canada. All local officials must be elected in Red River, and both the legislature and the courts must be bilingual. There would be a free homestead and land pre-emption law. Red River was to have fair representation in the Canadian Parliament, and all "privileges, customs and usages existing at the time of the transfer" must be continued. The English-speaking delegates thought this list was fair, and moved sending delegates to negotiate with McDougall.

But Riel shook his head. "We Métis will accept no promises made by McDougall himself," he said. "He must have these rights guaranteed by an act of the Canadian Parliament. Only then will we admit him into Red River."

James Ross threw up his hands. "That's impossible! How can we present the man with terms like that?" he demanded.

Riel's temper flared. "Go, return peacefully to your farms," he scornfully told the anglophone delegates. "Rest in the arms of your wives. Give that example to your children. But watch us act. We are going to work and obtain the guarantee of our rights and of yours. You will come to share them in the end."

The council disbanded. Riel's first attempt to unite French-speakers and English-speakers had failed, but there was something that none of them knew yet, not even McDougall in Pembina. The Canadian government had postponed the takeover of Rupert's Land because of the Métis resistance. So McDougall's proclamation was null and void, though news of this would not reach the settlement for two more weeks. There was now no government at all in Red River.

Meanwhile, Riel discovered that McDougall had authorized Colonel Dennis to issue a call to arms, urging loyal men to resist the Métis. Louis mustered more men and sent them to confiscate all the weapons and ammunition in Winnipeg. When a defiant group of Canadians gathered in John Schultz's store, Riel ordered armed Métis to surround them. Two cannons were wheeled up and aimed at the building. Before them all, Riel threw Dennis' call to arms on the ground and stamped on it. Sullenly, the Canadians surrendered. They were marched off as prisoners to Fort Garry.

∽

On December 8, Riel issued the "Declaration of the People of Rupert's Land and the North-West," which established a provisional government. Two days later, he ordered an official celebration. An excited crowd gathered in the main square of Fort Garry to watch as the Union Jack was hauled down. Then the white, blue, and green flag of the provisional government sailed up the flagpole. It was greeted by cheers, a *feu de joie*, and the tootling of the St. Boniface Boys' Bugle Band. Though John Bruce was declared the president of the new government, it was Louis who gave a rousing speech in French, English, and Cree.

"Always remember we are still loyal subjects of the Queen," he concluded.

Later that month, Riel replaced Bruce as president, and Louis Schmidt became the official secretary of the new government. One of Riel's main problems now was how to pay and provision his men. So, on December 22, he seized the Hudson's Bay Company's cash. Another problem was security. He offered to release his Canadian prisoners if they would swear loyalty to his government or at least promise not to take up arms against it. They refused, so for the moment he kept them locked up.

But Riel's biggest problem was Canada, because the Canadian government did not wish to negotiate directly with "rebels." Instead, the prime minister, Sir John A. Macdonald, sent Donald Smith to Red River. Officially, he was there to investigate the situation and explain the Canadian government's good intentions. Behind the scenes, he was supposed to bribe Riel's opponents to work against the provisional government.

Smith arrived on December 27, and Riel desperately wanted to know whether he had powers to negotiate an agreement between Red River and Canada.

But, "I will reveal my commission only at a mass meeting," Smith told him stiffly.

Riel hesitated. It was risky – Smith might turn public opinion against him. And Louis knew that if Smith really did have the power to negotiate, the English-speakers would support him. But what choice did he have? "Very well," he agreed.

The mass meeting was held on January 19, 1870. The day dawned bright but bitterly cold. From the window of the fort, Louis could see at least a thousand people packed into the square. Bundled against the cold in fur coats or dark blue capotes with colourful woollen sashes, they stamped their feet and blew on their hands to keep their circulation going. Many dashed indoors now and then for warming snorts of liquor.

Riel began the proceedings. "I nominate Thomas Bunn to lead the meeting," he said. There was a buzz of approval, for Bunn was an English-speaker.

Then Smith began to speak. He said nothing about negotiating, just repeated the same stale promises about Canada's good intentions. People had heard all that before, and after five hours in the cold, they grew restless. Hecklers called for the release of the Canadian prisoners.

"Not just yet," replied Riel.

The next day, even more people showed up. Smith gave another long speech, then Louis stepped forward.

"We have all heard what Mr. Smith has to say," he said. "Now we need to discuss matters and decide what to do. I move that twenty French-speaking and twenty English-speaking representatives be elected to meet on the 25th of this month to discuss what would be best for the welfare of the country."

The motion was carried. Then, before the meeting broke up, Riel spoke again. "I came here with fear," he admitted. "We are not yet enemies but we came very near being so. As soon as we understood each other, we joined in demanding our just rights. We claim no half-rights, mind you, but all the rights we are entitled to. Those rights will be set forth by our representatives, and what is more, gentlemen, we will get them!"

Men cheered and threw their fur caps in the air. Louis had his English-speakers back.

∞

But Riel was bitterly disappointed by some of the results in the election that followed. Although Louis himself was easily elected, Americans had packed the meeting in one parish and elected two delegates. Worse, a group led by Charles Nolin, Louis's cousin by marriage, worked against his supporters, and elected three of the twenty francophone delegates.

The Convention of Forty met on January 26. Riel, Ross, Nolin, and three others formed a committee to draw up a new List of Rights. The document included guarantees for local customs, usages, and languages, and for land rights. Everyone agreed to these demands.

Then Louis stood up. "Gentlemen, I move that Red River enter Canada as a province, not a mere territory," he announced. "This will give us better control over natural resources and public lands. I also move that the deal between the Hudson's Bay Company and Canada should be set aside. Canada must negotiate directly with the people of Red River."

There was a stunned silence. No one else was ready to go that far. In the vote that followed, Nolin's group helped the anglophone delegates defeat both motions.

Louis was furious. "The devil take it. We must win!" he raged. "It is a shame to have lost it; and it was a greater shame because it was lost by those traitors!" And he pointed at Nolin and his supporters.

"I was not sent here, Mr. Riel, to vote at your dictation," Nolin shot back.

"Your influence is finished in this country!" thundered Riel. "The provisional government will add provincial status to the List of Rights anyway!"

Convinced that the Hudson's Bay Company was behind Nolin's opposition, Louis put the bedridden Mactavish under armed guard and arrested the Company's second-in-command. A.G.B. Bannatyne, one of Louis's strongest supporters among the English-speaking mixed-bloods, went to the fort to see the Mactavish family, and Riel clapped him in jail too.

Then Riel's men went after Nolin, who was guarded by his brothers. Guns were drawn on both sides, but luckily misfired.

On February 7, Riel clashed with Donald Smith in the Convention.

"It's clear, sir," he said at last, "that you have no power to guarantee a single item on this List of Rights!"

Smith could not deny that this was true. "But the Canadian government is willing to receive delegates from Red River to discuss terms," he said.

"Good," said Riel. "But somebody has to mind the country while these negotiations go on." And he asked for English-speaking delegates to be elected to join the Métis in his government. "The provisional government has accomplished some good," he pleaded. "Help it do more."

In the end they decided that the new provisional government would have twelve Métis and twelve anglophone members. In return, Riel was to release his prisoners. Louis refused to be one of the delegates to Canada. As the leader of the Resistance, he might be arrested. And who else in Red River could hold the provisional government together until negotiations were completed? So he chose instead to be the president of the new government. Father Ritchot, Judge John Black, and Alfred H. Scott were chosen to carry Red River's demands to Ottawa.

On the night of February 10, Riel ordered fireworks set off to celebrate. He grinned as the rockets spangled the night sky with coloured stars, for the fireworks belonged to Schultz and had been intended to welcome McDougall. Most of Red River then began a whoop-up, with *feux de joie*, shouting, singing, and drinking that lasted until four in the morning. Louis did not join the party. But he tossed down "a good horn of brandy" with Mr. Bannatyne when he let him out of the Fort Garry calaboose.

Riel and his **Métis** advisors in 1869.

6

Father of a Province

While Riel was forming the provisional government, there had been two daring jailbreaks from
Fort Garry. On January 9, Charles Mair, a tall red-
haired Irishman named Thomas Scott, and a small
group of Riel's other prisoners climbed out a window.
They fled to the settlement of Portage la Prairie, west
of Red River, where they began raising volunteers to
help free the remaining prisoners. Then, on January
23, Riel's arch-enemy John Schultz also escaped, slid-
ing down a rope tied from strips of a buffalo robe.

"Find him!" ordered Riel, white with fury.

They scoured the settlement, but Schultz was
holed up in Kildonan, north of Winnipeg. He, too,
began organizing resistance to Riel.

On February 12, Riel released sixteen more Canadians from jail. But that very day he learned that a hundred men had marched from Portage la Prairie to free the prisoners. On February 15, he watched them pass Fort Garry. He heard that they had ransacked a house in Winnipeg where he stayed sometimes, then moved north to Kildonan to meet volunteers led by Schultz. Meanwhile, Louis had already released the last batch of Canadian prisoners. Hearing this, most of the volunteers at Kildonan disbanded.

But the hotheads from Portage la Prairie insisted on marching back the way they had come, right under the noses of the Métis. As they floundered through the snow, Louis sent horsemen to capture the lot. He clapped Major Boulton, their leader, in irons and threatened to execute him. Donald Smith and leading citizens of Red River arrived to plead for his life, and Riel was quick to gain an advantage. He would spare Boulton, he told Smith, if the anglophone parishes kept their promise to elect delegates to the joint provisional government. They agreed, and Boulton's life was saved.

Now, only the willpower of Louis Riel was holding the provisional government together. The pressure on him was intense, and he faced serious problems. The cells of the Fort bulged with prisoners again. What should he do with them? Supplies were running short, so he confiscated the last provisions of the Hudson's Bay Company and had its cattle herds slaughtered. He also feared another uprising, or an invasion from Canada. So he sent word to the Métis wintering in the West that they might be needed to fight later on. On

February 24, he fell ill with "brain fever." But he drove himself back to work in just a few days.

∞

Meanwhile, one of Riel's prisoners was causing serious problems. Thomas Scott, who had escaped on January 9, had been recaptured on February 17. His temper was as hot as his hair was red, and he was foul-mouthed. He despised the Métis as rebels, and cursed his guards. They demanded that he be punished. Louis was involved in at least one of Scott's scuffles with his guards and Scott insulted him in person. So on March 3, Riel allowed Scott to be tried before a Métis council. At the trial, Scott had no legal defence, and he was not present when evidence was given against him. Riel did not sit on the council, but he gave evidence against Scott. He also acted as translator and summarized for the accused in English what had been said in French. The council voted four to three to execute Scott the next day.

Again Donald Smith and others begged Riel for clemency.

"The one great merit of your insurrection," Smith pleaded, "is that so far, it has been bloodless. Don't now strain it – burden it with what will be considered a horrible crime."

But Riel refused to change the sentence. "We must make Canada respect us," he replied.

Thomas Scott was shot outside the walls of Fort Garry on March 4, 1870. The execution horrified the people of Red River. Riel was respected now. He was also feared.

∞

On March 9, 1870, the joint provisional government met for the first time.

"The people now have, for the first time in the history of this land, a voice in the direction of public affairs," Riel proudly pointed out to the councillors. "What Red River needs now is unity and a spirit of conciliation."

Riel began work on the List of Rights to be presented to Canada. As president, he changed the terms to suit his own views and those of his closest advisors. He added the provision that Red River would enter Canada as a province. He also demanded a full amnesty for all who had participated in the Resistance. Another change, the demand for a separate (religious) school system for the new province, may have been suggested by Bishop Taché. None of these new clauses was ever approved by the general council of the provisional government. By the end of March, all the delegates had left for Canada.

Weeks passed, and Red River basked in a beautiful spring. The sun shone through the windows of *Monsieur le président*'s apartment in Fort Garry, glinting on the glossy furniture the Métis had confiscated from William McDougall. Smiling, Louis ran a finger along the polished arm of the chair he sat in. He knew very well that people criticized him for using the furniture, and accused him of pomp and vanity. But why not enjoy it? Was it not his due as the head of government, an outward sign of his accomplishments?

He had had reports that the negotiations in Ottawa were going well. Father Ritchot wrote that they had gained much of what they had asked for. Red River and a small area of territory around it would enter the Canadian Confederation as the Province of Manitoba. Most of the other demands were granted too, including separate schools. On the other hand, Louis had wanted his new province to control its public lands, but this had been refused. Instead, 1,400,000 acres (3,459,000 hectares) of land would be set aside for the Métis and their children. The amnesty was another sticking point. It was not included in the Manitoba Act that the Canadian Parliament passed on May 12, 1870.

But at least life in Red River was going back to normal. Riel had had the Union Jack raised over Fort Garry again, with the flag of the provisional government below it. All the prisoners had been released, and he had squeezed a loan out of Mactavish for running the government. Now the Hudson's Bay Company was back in business. The Métis winterers were bringing their furs in to trade. The voyageurs were heading west toward the Saskatchewan, and the ox carts were jolting south to St. Paul again.

On April 9, he had issued a "Proclamation to the People of the North-West," announcing the end of martial law. Thanks to the provisional government, he had reminded people, they now enjoyed responsible government. Roads were open, and mail would not be censored. Trade would resume. There would be amnesty for all. Now people could stop fretting about politics and go back to more usual worries about floods and grasshoppers, Riel thought hopefully.

True, there were difficulties. For one thing, the members of the council had found out about the changes he had made to the List of Rights. They were furious at not having been consulted, and he had to smooth their ruffled feathers. And then there was O'Donoghue. Riel sighed. The Irishman had been one of the first to rally to the Métis cause. But O'Donoghue sympathized with the Fenians, Irish Catholic agitators who opposed the British. He wanted Red River to be annexed by the United States, and accused Riel of being pro-British.

And there were far worse problems. His old enemies, Schultz and Mair, had returned to Ontario. Riel realized now that the execution of Thomas Scott had handed them a powerful weapon against him. In Ontario they had orchestrated a campaign of mass meetings, newspaper articles, placards, and torchlight parades, damning him and the Métis as bloodthirsty murderers. To make things worse, Scott had turned out to be a member of the Orange Order, a Protestant anti-Catholic organization with deep roots in Ontario. So anti-Catholic bigotry was also being roused against the Métis.

Riel's brow darkened as he jumped up and paced restlessly back and forth. He knew from newspaper reports that the people of Quebec were on his side. But Schultz and Mair had turned half the population of Canada against him! And then there was the military expedition Father Ritchot had warned him about. The Canadian government said it was sending troops under Colonel Garnet Wolseley on a mission of peace. Was it a lie? And what about the amnesty? The Scott affair made it more important than ever now. Without it, he and other Métis might be tried for murder. How he longed to talk with Father Ritchot!

On June 17, a young Métis hunter asked to see Riel.

"*Monsieur le président*, my name is Gabriel Dumont," he said. "I've ridden all the way from the Saskatchewan territory to see you. I have five hundred good men there who will come to fight for you if you need them."

Riel clapped him on the shoulder. "*Mille mercis*," he said. "But our negotiations with Canada seem to be going well."

"Remember, we will come if you summon us," promised Dumont.

That very day, Father Ritchot returned, and hurried to Riel. He went straight to the subject of the amnesty.

"Prime Minister Macdonald claims he can do nothing," he told Louis. "He says because Red River was not part of Canada when the Resistance began, any amnesty must come from the British government. But that's not the real reason. The hullabaloo in Ontario about the Scott affair has frightened Macdonald and the Conservative party. They fear losing the next election if they issue an amnesty."

"It's that bad, is it?"

Father Ritchot nodded. "So I had a meeting with the Governor General and a British envoy. Both promised me that a full and complete amnesty will come through. So did Sir George Cartier. He said it's a sure thing."

"I pray that's so," replied Louis. But he felt a pang of uneasiness.

On the sultry night of June 25, amid much swatting of mosquitoes, the council of the provisional government, now renamed the legislative assembly, accepted the Manitoba Act unanimously. Riel felt a fierce surge of pride. This brand-new province with responsible government was his creation, his alone. And his Métis people had their land grant. That should give them some security from the flood of settlers that would surely swamp Manitoba sooner or later.

Riel's job now, as he saw it, was to run Red River in the name of the provisional government until the takeover date, July 15. After that he would govern in the interest of Canada until the arrival of the new lieutenant-governor, A.G. Archibald.

"I will keep what is mine until the proper government arrives," he told Joseph Dubuc, an old friend from his Montreal days. He could only hope that Archibald would arrive before the military expedition. That way there would be less chance of trouble.

In Red River, the lovely spring became a hot, dry summer. Burning winds scorched the prairie, and grasshoppers chirred in the fields. As the heat built, so did Riel's feeling of tension. July 15 came and went, and Manitoba was now a province of Canada. He knew that the remaining Canadians in Red River, still cowed, were muttering that the military expedition was bound to hang "a few of the French party." And Riel's old Métis enemies were grumbling that he had brought trouble on them all.

Métis labourers had been hired by the Canadian government to guide the troops and clear a road for them. They sent word to Riel that the Canadian soldiers were threatening bloodthirsty revenge for Scott's death. But what could he do? The loyal voyageurs and tripmen were far away from the settlement. He could not keep the troops out of Red River even if he had wanted to. More weeks passed, and Lieutenant-Governor Archibald did not appear. There was no word of the amnesty.

On August 23, Riel received word that the troops were just thirty-two kilometres away. That night, he and several men rode through driving rain to scout out the enemy. Peering through the downpour, they saw the winking eyes of many campfires.

"Pack all our papers. Get them out of here!" Riel ordered Louis Schmidt when he got back. Pale with fright, Schmidt did his best.

Riel took off his wet overcoat and shoes and wrapped himself in heavy blankets. He slept only three-quarters of an hour. Dawn was breaking, and rain still poured down. He wolfed down some cold meat, but it lay heavy on his stomach.

There was a thud of feet on the stairs, and James Stewart, an English-speaking settler, burst into the room. "The troops are just a few kilometres away," he yelled. "You are going to be lynched!"

"Everybody out!" ordered Riel. "*Sauve qui peut!*"

He and O'Donoghue were the last to leave. Already they could see soldiers in the outskirts of the village.

"Come on!" urged O'Donoghue. "We'll cross the river to Bishop Taché's house."

But Riel lingered not far from the fort. Close enough to see the troops rush in and come out again empty-handed. Close enough to flinch as they fired a twenty-one-gun salute.

"Riel's bandits have fled," shouted an officer in a gold-braided uniform.

Yet Riel was there.

Part Three
Embers

The execution of Thomas Scott in 1870. Such dramatic
images roused emotions against Riel in Ontario.
Canadian Illustrated News, 17 September, 1870,
Volume II, Number 12. 1869-1883.

Cartoon showing Riel fleeing Fort Garry
as Colonel Wolseley's men arrive.

7

Dispossessed and Exiled

"**M**ust you go away, Louis?" Alexandre, his "little pet" tugged at his big brother's sleeve.

"I must, *mon petit.*"

Riel had gone straight home from Bishop Taché's house, but he knew he must not linger. Already Wolseley's troops would be baying on his trail. But what would happen to his family now? Surely *le bon Dieu* will keep them safe! he thought, embracing them.

He, O'Donoghue, and Lépine rode for the border. But that night their horses wandered off while they slept. Fearful of being caught by Canadian soldiers on the main Pembina trail, they decided to cross the river. They pulled down fence rails and bound them together with strips torn from their clothing to make a rough raft. Louis lost a shoe during the crossing and had to plod on for almost fifty kilometres barefoot.

After three days, hungry and weary, the three reached the house of a friendly Métis at Pembina, on the American side of the border. But Louis still feared for his life and wanted to press on. He accepted only a meal of dried fish and a pair of shoes, then set out with a guide for St. Joseph.

"Tell them that that he who ruled in Fort Garry a few days ago is now a homeless wanderer with nothing to eat but two dried suckers," he joked bitterly to a Métis they met on the trail.

At St. Joseph, Riel found refuge with Father LeFloch, who had once been his teacher at Red River. The first thing Louis did was send Sara a message that he was safe. He would not return, he said, "until matters are arranged." Over the next few weeks, Father LeFloch and Bishop Taché advised him to be patient, and Louis tried. Still fearful of assassins, he moved around, sleeping in different houses.

One night, Lépine and O'Donoghue came to meet him. Lépine was as loyal as always, but the Irishman was in a bitter mood.

"You should have fought Wolseley when you had the chance!" he accused.

"Fought him how?" replied Riel wearily. "With what troops?"

"We could have taken to the woods and picked them off one by one," said O'Donoghue.

"But we couldn't have kept them out of Red River. And Manitoba is part of Canada now. It would have meant fighting the British."

"Ah, you always were a coward and a traitor," snarled O'Donoghue. "Fight me, then, if you won't fight the British!" And he struck Riel across the face.

Louis's face flamed with rage. "Remember this," he snapped. "You are not Métis. My people will always choose me over you!"

But things were bad in Red River, he knew. Canadian troops, frustrated in their desire to lynch him, roamed drunk and disorderly through the settlement. They persecuted any Métis they met, killing several and badly beating others. Louis shuddered when he heard that women as well as men were abused. To make matters worse, John Schultz was back, stirring up bigotry and racism among Canadian settlers.

Riel arranged a meeting at St. Vital on September 17. O'Donoghue attended, and the two men eyed each other warily.

"We can all agree on the perfidious treachery of the Canadian government," Riel said. "It promised an amnesty, but has not sent it. And the government allows the violence to continue. So let us send a petition to the president of the United States, listing our grievances. Let us ask him to intercede with Queen Victoria on our behalf."

"I say the British have had their chance," cried O'Donoghue. "Let's petition for annexation by the United States!"

"No!" shouted Riel.

The two men glared at each other. And when it came to the vote, the Métis supported Riel.

Louis stayed at St. Joseph throughout the fall and winter. His sister Marie arrived to look after him, and his brother Charles came along. Riel heard that Sara was safe too. She had been recalled to the mother house of the Grey Nuns in St. Boniface. In January she wrote that the nuns had taken the other Riel girls into their boarding school. He blessed them for offering charity and protection to his hard-pressed family. But he worried about his younger brothers and his mother.

Meanwhile, Joseph Dubuc and other friends suggested he might run in the upcoming provincial elections. Who had a better right than he to become premier of the new province of Manitoba? they demanded. Riel refused, fearing to provoke the Canadian government and hold up the amnesty, but he encouraged his friends to run. With Métis sympathizers dominating the new legislature, it would be that much easier for him to become premier once the amnesty came through. Yet when Schmidt and Dubuc and fifteen other "Rielists" were elected, he felt a flash of resentment. Why should he have to sit by while they shared in the government of the province he had created?

In February 1871, Riel fell seriously ill. He burned with fever, and his joints became painfully swollen. He may have had rheumatic fever. Julie Riel arrived to nurse him, and slowly he recovered. On May 3, Louis returned quietly to St. Vital. The news spread by word of mouth throughout the French parishes, and soon crowds gathered at the little farmhouse near the river to greet the Métis leader. Safe among his people, Louis kept a low profile. He was growing more and more alarmed, though, that the

Canadian government was not keeping the terms of the Manitoba Act. Métis land grants had not been finalized, yet newcomers were being encouraged to grab some of the best lands in the province. Riel drew up a letter of protest, which he sent to Dubuc. But he spoke in public only once, to honour Bishop Taché, who had been made an archbishop.

∞

That autumn, Riel heard through Father Ritchot that O'Donoghue was planning to invade Manitoba with a ragtag army of Fenians and set up a republic. So when Archbishop Taché sent for him, he knew what was on his mind.

"Lieutenant-Governor Archibald is worried," the archbishop said. "He fears that the Métis will join O'Donoghue if he invades Canada."

"Would you blame them if they did," said Riel. "considering the way they have been treated by the government?"

"Are you associated with O'Donoghue in this matter?" the archbishop demanded.

"No," replied Riel. Then he shrugged. "But I am not sure what I should do. You know perfectly well that my life is not safe. I may go in the front and fight against the Fenians, and I am sure to be killed by those behind me. But you can rest assured there is not the slightest danger of me or any one of my friends going with the Fenians."

On September 28, he called a meeting to discuss matters. The Métis must remain unified, he said. And he moved that those at the meeting "should pronounce themselves in favour of the advantages already possessed by the Manitoba Bill." When O'Donoghue sent messengers asking the Métis to join him, nobody did. And the Métis began drilling in St. Boniface in support of the Manitoba government. In early October Riel heard that O'Donoghue and his conspirators had been arrested by American forces.

On October 8, Riel drew up his men in ranks on a field at St. Boniface. French-speaking members of the new legislative assembly were there to inspect the troops. With them was Lieutenant-Governor Archibald. There were cheers, and guns fired in salute.

"This is one of our leaders. Thanks to him you have such loyal troops," said one of the legislators.

"Sir," said Louis, holding out his hand.

Though no names had been mentioned, Archibald knew perfectly well who this man with the challenging gaze was. With a nod, he shook his hand.

Riel eagerly read accounts of the incident in the papers. Of course Canadians in Red River and Ontario howled in protest. But most Manitobans thought the lieutenant-governor had done well. Surely the longed-for amnesty would arrive now! Riel told himself. Had he not proved his loyalty in time of need? But the hullabaloo about the handshake caused hatred against him to flare up again in Winnipeg. On December 8, while he was away at a meeting, a band of masked men broke into the Riel homestead and ransacked it.

"One of them put a gun to my head. He asked me where you were," Marie told him, trembling. "Of course I didn't tell him!" she added, with a toss of her head.

Mon Dieu! thought Riel. Is it safe for me to stay? Is it safe for my family?

∞

One day Archbishop Taché summoned Riel and Lépine. "Prime Minister Macdonald has asked me to give you a message," he said. "He wishes you both to leave the country for a time."

"Until the Orange Protestants of Ontario stop baying for our heads?" asked Riel bitterly.

"Until things quiet down," agreed the archbishop. "If you will stay away for a year, he offers you money to live on."

"Does he think he can buy us?" snapped Louis, and Lépine growled his agreement.

"He knows you are both poor men," said the archbishop smoothly. "If you agree to go, there will be money to help your families too."

Riel and Lépine exchanged glances. It was true that they hardly dared leave their farms. In the end, both agreed to go. They left under escort on February 23, 1872, bound for St. Paul. There, Riel settled down to write a memorandum about the Scott affair, to be published in a Quebec newspaper.

But even in St. Paul their enemies shadowed them. They learned that the Ontario government had offered a bounty of five thousand dollars for their arrest. Then John Schultz showed up in St. Paul. Men came to Riel and swore that Schultz had tried to bribe them to steal his papers. Riel and Lépine fled to a nearby town, but there they overheard men plotting to murder them for the reward.

Lépine decided to return to Red River. "If I'm going to die, let it be in my own country," he said.

Lonely and bitter, Riel finished his manuscript. He had been waiting for two years now and had even accepted exile, but still no amnesty had come. It was time to act, he decided. His friends wanted him to run in the upcoming federal election – he would do it!

∞

Riel began campaigning in the francophone parishes of Red River. He expected to win Provencher riding handily. Louis imagined himself standing before the Canadian Parliament explaining Métis grievances and justifying his actions, and his spirits kindled. If they would only listen, he knew the amnesty would be granted. He was sure of victory, but then Cartier was defeated in the federal election in Quebec. Archbishop Taché and others reminded Riel that Cartier had promised the amnesty. If Louis allowed Cartier to win in his place, the great man would be in his debt. The archbishop also passed on messages from Prime Minister Macdonald that seemed to promise movement on the amnesty if Riel cooperated. So on September 13, 1872, Louis refused the nomination in Provencher and Cartier was elected by acclamation. Louis and his supporters quickly sent Cartier a pointed telegram, reminding him of "the cause entrusted to you."

But the amnesty did not come, and Riel's thoughts turned again to politics as a way of putting pressure on the Canadian government. If the people of Manitoba elected him, the longed-for amnesty would surely be granted! So he spoke to the member of the provincial legislature for St. Vital, who agreed to step aside so Riel could run in his place. His friends warned him that if he tried to carry out this plan, warrants would be issued for his and Lépine's arrest. And sure enough, on December 3 two men tried to arrest them on the charge of the murder of Thomas Scott. He and Lépine escaped, but once more they had to go into hiding. The will-o'-the wisp of the amnesty was still beyond Riel's grasp.

∞

In January 1873, Riel's sister Marie died. Shaken, Riel went on a religious retreat during March and April. Sara, who had become a missionary at Île-à-la-Crosse in the Saskatchewan country, wrote letters urging him to think again of becoming a priest. But in May, Riel learned that Cartier had died. Now there would be a byelection in Provencher riding. Louis decided to run, but once again his enemies tried to stop him. In September, new warrants were sworn out against him and Lépine. Though Lépine was arrested, Riel escaped. Guarded by loyal supporters, he hid in the woods across the river from St. Norbert.

One evening his friend Dubuc watched him warming himself over a campfire. "King David, in the Bible, also had to hide from his foes," he joked.

Louis looked up, smiling. "David…" he mused. "A name of renown."

On October 13 Riel was elected by acclamation. His friends spirited him out of Red River and sent him off to Montreal.

He received a hero's welcome. Former schoolmates – Dr. Ernest Lachapelle, Jean-Baptiste-Romuald Fiset – rallied around. Old friends like Rodrigue Masson introduced him to people who mattered. One of these was Alphonse Desjardins, the owner of *Le Nouveau Monde*. His newspaper had published Louis's first letter from Red River and backed the Métis cause. Another was Honoré Mercier, an important politician.

"You are the very symbol of our culture," they told him. "Attacks on you are attacks on all French Canadians."

"I know the support of the people of Quebec is my only hope of gaining the amnesty," Riel said. "And the plight of my Métis people is part of the greater struggle between English-speaking and French-speaking people in Canada."

On a dark autumn day, Riel and some supporters met in a house in Hull, across the river from Ottawa. Haunted by the thought of Lépine in prison, Louis wanted to take his seat in Parliament at once, and then convince the government to grant an amnesty for him and Lépine before his friend came to trial. But gazing at the looming grey towers of Parliament, he felt his heart sink.

"My enemies are there, waiting to seize me," he said. "Will I even get a chance to speak?"

So he returned to Montreal. Not long afterward, the government was dissolved, and a new election was called. So Riel went to New York State, where he could rest in safety. In December, 1873, he visited Father Fabien Barnabé, who lived in the village of Keeseville, one of many "little Canadas" where French Canadians had come to live and work in the United States. Father Barnabé lived with his mother and his sister Evelina.

"It's so good to feel part of a family again," Louis told them. But his mind was already on the next election. In preparation, he wrote another defence of his actions in 1869-70, explaining the execution of Scott and the Canadian government's promises of an amnesty. By mid-January, he was back in Montreal. The election was to be held on February 13, 1874. Riel could not campaign in person but that didn't matter to his loyal supporters in Red River. He was elected by 195 votes to 68.

And this time I'll take my seat in Parliament, he promised himself.

∞

On March 26, 1874, snow crunched under Riel's polished boots as he walked toward the Parliament Buildings. In the crowded lobby, he glanced around nervously. But no one paid any attention to the bearded stranger with Monsieur Fiset, the member for Rimouski.

"You must take the oath of allegiance," Fiset told him. And he led Riel to the office of the Clerk of the House of Commons.

The busy little bureaucrat behind the desk barely glanced up. "Another new member?" he asked, as Riel stepped forward.

The clerk read the oath aloud, and Riel replied, "I do swear that I will be faithful and bear true allegiance to Her Majesty, Queen Victoria." Then he leaned forward and signed the Parliamentary register with a flourish.

Just as Riel and Fiset were leaving, the clerk's eye fell on the signature. "Louis Riel!" he cried, jumping to his feet.

From the doorway, Louis gave him a cheeky bow.

For the next several days, Louis gleefully followed the newspaper accounts of his adventure. Sensation-seekers had packed the Visitors' Gallery in the House of Commons wondering if the outlaw would take his seat. An amnesty bill for those involved in the Red River Resistance was being voted on, and Rodrigue Masson and Joseph-Alfred Mousseau moved that Riel and Lépine be included in it. They were voted down. The next day, Ontario politicians had demanded that Riel take his seat or be expelled. But Louis, who had returned to Montreal, did not appear. On April 9, the House voted to expel him from Parliament.

But Riel had created the public relations sensation he wanted. And what would be the point of risking jail by trying to take his seat? he told himself. A Select Committee of the House of Commons had been created to investigate the events of 1869-70 and the question of the amnesty, and his recent pamphlet was being widely discussed. On May 27 Louis wrote to Dubuc, "The fact is, our cause is making progress... our cause is shaking the Canadian Confederation from one end of the country to the other. It is gaining strength daily." Of course, now that he was expelled, his seat in

Provencher was vacant. Why not run for it again, just to underscore his popularity?

∽

While waiting for the election, Louis resumed his wandering life. He went to Keeseville in June for a visit, and there he flirted with Evelina Barnabé. He had always yearned for a family of his own, and hoped to find a pious girl who might become his wife. Now he had met one. It didn't hurt that she was slender, blonde and blue-eyed. And her glances told him that she returned his interest.

But the question of the amnesty and the upcoming trial of Ambroise Lépine preyed on his mind. In the "little Canadas" dotted around New England, Riel stayed in the houses of priests sympathetic to his cause and gave fiery speeches at protest meetings demanding the amnesty for himself and his friend. Homesick, he travelled west as far as St. Paul, but he heard that Schultz, his old enemy, had been seen there, and soon returned to the East. In Quebec, he visited influential people who could help his cause, including Bishop Bourget of Montreal. On September 3, 1874, he was again elected to Parliament by the stubbornly loyal voters of Provencher riding.

In November Riel was deeply shocked when Lépine was convicted of murder and sentenced to be hanged. He had believed no Manitoba jury would convict him. Reading the protests in the French-Canadian press, he comforted himself that at least the people of Quebec were on his side. Heartsick, he barnstormed throughout New England, rousing public opinion against the verdict. Then he went to Washington, D.C., to stay with Edmund Mallet, an influential French-Canadian friend.

While he was there, he had a remarkable experience. On the 18th of December he climbed a mountain not far from the city. Suddenly a burning cloud appeared before him. From the depths of it a spirit – the same spirit who showed himself to Moses, Louis was sure – spoke to him, saying "Rise up, Louis David Riel, you have a mission to fulfill." Stretching out his arms and bowing his head, Riel received the heavenly message.

∽

In January 1875, the Governor General of Canada commuted Lépine's sentence to two years' imprisonment. Riel was overjoyed. Then in February, he picked up a newspaper and his heart beat faster as the words "amnesty" and "Red River" leaped out at him. An amnesty had been proposed for everyone involved in the Red River Resistance! But his heart sank as he read on. He and Lépine would only be amnestied after five years' banishment, and their political rights would be suspended for the rest of their lives. Despite the protests of Riel's friends in Parliament, the measure had passed. And on February 24, he was again expelled from the House of Commons.

The longed-for amnesty came as a cruel blow. *Five more years!* Hadn't he already been a fugitive for five years? As an exile, how could he earn a living and help his family? Riel wondered. And barred from his rightful place in politics, how could he fulfill his mission to help his people? Sorrowfully, he penned a poem:

> Far from one's homeland
> Having friends is in vain.
> For despite their tenderness
> One's soul is ever sad.
> Friends, forgive me if your kind hearts
> Are afflicted by the tears I shed.
> Every moment of the day my yearning soul
> Sends its thoughts far away
> To the place where I was born...

Restless, he resumed his American travels, staying at the homes of friends, making speeches. At meeting after meeting in the "little Canadas" he protested against his banishment. And he begged the French Canadians there to emigrate to the North-West Territories.

"It is the only way French-Canadian culture can compete there against the flood of English-speaking immigrants from Ontario," he told them. "Go, make new lives for yourselves!"

People applauded, but Riel feared they would not heed him. The North-West was too far away for them, the life there too harsh.

Late that fall, he dashed west to Indianapolis, to visit an influential American senator. Now that Canada had turned its back on him, he had been mulling over plans to invade Manitoba and set up a new government in the North-West. He was convinced that the Métis would support him. He needed money, though, and a promise that the Americans would back him against Canada. But the senator was unimpressed. In December, he returned to Washington, D.C., where he spoke with President Ulysses S. Grant.

"We will establish a Métis and French-Canadian republic in Manitoba, and another republic for Irish Catholics farther west," he told Grant. "Tens of thousands of supporters will rally to my cause!"

The President listened politely, but promised nothing.

With nowhere left to turn, Riel struggled to fan the embers of his hopes. Politics had failed him, true. But he consoled himself with the memory of his vision on the mountaintop. Had not God himself told him he still had a mission to fulfill? And since then had Bishop Bourget not written him a letter echoing those very words? Louis brooded on Bourget's letter. He carried it over his heart, and placed it at the head of his bed at night. His only comfort now was the burning belief that his true mission would soon be revealed.

8

Prophet of the New World

O n December 8, 1875, Riel attended mass at St. Patrick's Church in Washington, D.C. As he followed the beloved words of the mass, he could not help thinking wistfully that it was six years to the day since he had proclaimed the provisional government in Red River. Suddenly a feeling of extreme joy seized him, and an ecstatic smile spread across his face. A small boy beside him stared up at him wide-eyed, so Louis covered his mouth and cheeks with his handkerchief. Moments later, his mood swung into sorrow so deep that he struggled to suppress tears and keep from crying out. In minutes that feeling, too, passed.

Riel was sure this experience was the beginning of his new mission. Over the next few days, he had other

This photograph was taken after Riel
left the asylum at Longue Pointe and
was on his way to Keeseville, New York.

powerful spiritual feelings. He believed the Holy Spirit spoke to him, and he saw a vision of the Virgin Mary. Usually quiet and devout, he burned with excitement and became very talkative.

"I am a prophet!" he told his friends joyfully.

Had Louis been living in a traditional aboriginal society, his mood swings, visions, and strange behaviour might have been seen as the beginning of a vocation as a shaman, a spiritual guide of his people. But living as he did in a modern society, his behaviour was interpreted as insanity.

Edmond Mallet, at whose home he was staying, feared Riel was going mad. Unable to look after Louis himself, he took him to Father Primeau in Worcester, Massachusetts. There Riel stayed for eight days. At times he seemed his normal self. Then he would be caught up in excitement again and talk wildly of his mission.

"Please," he begged Father Primeau. "Let me announce in Worcester what I will soon have to proclaim throughout the world, my mission as a prophet."

"My poor child!" said Father Primeau. "These are impossible illusions!"

Louis wept. "But we have to do miracles!" he protested.

Father Primeau decided to take Riel to stay with Father Richer in Suncook, New Hampshire. By now Louis was saying that he was one of a trinity of persecuted rulers, each represented by a bull. "The Comte de Chambord of France – he's a white bull. Don Carlos of Spain is a black one. I, the rightful leader of the Métis people, am a red bull!" he insisted. And all the way to Suncook on the train he snorted like a bull. Only severe glances from Father Primeau quieted him a little.

Riel spent twenty-five days with Father Richer. Sometimes he became calm, but then his hectic excitement would return. Hoping the loving household of Father Barnabé might help, Father Richer sent him to Keeseville, accompanied by a keeper. But poor Father Barnabé and his mother were overwhelmed. Riel couldn't sleep, and paced his room crying and howling. After ten awful days, Father Barnabé sent a telegram to John Lee, Louis's uncle, in Montreal. The night John Lee arrived, Riel spent hours bellowing like a bull. The next day he kept it up on the journey to Montreal, too.

"Do not laugh, I beg you! I am a prophet!" Louis cried, when other passengers sniggered at his odd behaviour.

Lee had to smuggle Riel into Canada because of his official exile. In Montreal, Louis went on crying and bellowing, and at times he fell into convulsions. Several times he tore his clothing and sheets to pieces.

"No, I'm not crazy!" he insisted. "Never say I'm crazy! I have a mission to perform and I am a prophet. You should say that you don't understand. I am sent by God."

∽

After several weeks, he grew a bit calmer. They began taking him out for carriage rides, and let him go to mass. But he created a scene in the church and had to be locked up again. At last the Lees sent for Dr. Ernest

Lachapelle, one Riel's old schoolmates. On March 6, 1876, Lee and Lachapelle took Riel for a carriage ride that ended at the Hospice de St. Jean-de-Dieu, at Longue Pointe. It was an asylum for the insane. To keep his identity secret, he was admitted as Louis R. David.

Louis entered quietly and was greeted at the door by Dr. Henry Howard, who knew who he really was.

The doctor held out his hand. "I am glad to see you, Mr. David," he said. "My name is Dr. Howard."

Louis started back. "Why do you call me David?" he demanded. "My name is Louis David Riel." Out of his coat pocket he pulled a little prayer book given him long ago by Sara. Pointing at the flyleaf, he added, "Look, there is my name, Louis Riel, written by my dear sister."

One of the nuns, fearing this evidence of Riel's identity, seized the book and ripped the page out. "You are only known here, sir, as Mr. David," she scolded him.

Louis's eyes blazed. She had torn Sara's book! He lunged at the nun, and had to be restrained.

The Hospice of St. Jean-de-Dieu was a pleasant-looking brick building set on 1500 hectares of garden and farmland. But Louis soon discovered that inside, it was overcrowded and dirty. He had to live in a tiny cell and eat miserable food. He was supposed to obey orders. If he didn't, his keepers handcuffed him or put him in a straitjacket. For serious punishment he was locked in a cell in the basement. From the moment he entered, he battled against his situation. Upset by conflicts with the staff, he smashed up his room and stripped naked, to the horror of the nuns. Disgusted by disorder in the chapel, he bellowed and turned things upside down. In his periods of calm, he pleaded with Dr. Howard to release him. He also showered Bishop Bourget with letters.

"The Holy Spirit pushes me with one hand and holds me back with the other," he wrote to him on April 20. "I feel at the same time crushed by a mountain and always on the point of taking flight on the wings of my mission. Oh, when will you come to help me?"

In time, his real identity became widely known in the asylum, and the nuns were worried that the vindictive Orangemen of Montreal would find out his whereabouts and attack them. Louis shared their fears. One night, he found that iron bars had been removed from his window. After that, he lived in terror of assassins.

On May 19, 1876, Riel was sent by steamboat to another asylum near Quebec City. His friends had to struggle to get him aboard. "I made myself go limp and they were hard put to hold me up. I looked at old Mousseau, his face covered with sweat, and I laughed up my sleeve," Louis wrote.

The Beauport asylum was not much better than the one at Longue Pointe. At first, Riel penned bitter poetry about his plight.

> Fools came to bundle me
> As they bind those possessed by the devil.
> Ignorant doctors prescribed as medicine
> Fetters of heavy leather like the harness of
> animals.

He also criticized the politicians who had driven him out of Parliament.

> Smoking your cigars,
> Ottawa, you lose your way.
> *Chorus*: Only too well do I know
> Your bad faith!
> Your men are shady characters
> Ferocious rascals.
> *Chorus*: Only too well do I know
> Your bad faith!
> You live a lie
> And your rage eats away at me.
> *Chorus*: Only too well do I know
> Your bad faith!

He was also angry at his old friend Joseph Dubuc, who had been elected in "his" riding of Provencher. He blamed Dubuc for not having done more to help Ambroise Lépine.

> Your conduct is brazen.
> The betrayed Métis are dying.
> You serve their odious tyrants.
> Saying in the depths of your shameless soul:
> "I do for them
> As much as any other coward would."

But as the months passed, Louis began to calm down. He talked less about being a prophet, and no longer claimed to be pope as he had done at first. He was allowed to attend mass again and to take communion. But he still spent much of his time writing about his mission. Day after day he wrote down the visions and revelations he received from God. From these he created a new faith called the Catholic, Apostolic, and Vital Church of the Shining Mountains. ("Vital" was a pun on the name St. Vital, his home.) The Church of the Shining Mountains was a revised form of the Roman Catholic religion, blended with Riel's spiritual faith in the Métis. He believed that the centre of the Catholic Church would move from Rome to Montreal, and Bishop Bourget would become the new pope. After 467 years, St. Vital would become the centre of the new religion. He wrote that the Métis were God's chosen people. In the vast territory of the North-West, they would carry out the mission of French Catholic culture in Canada, and many other peoples would come to join them. God, Riel believed, had chosen him as the prophet of the New World. His mission was to relay God's wishes to humankind. As he said in one of his poems,

> When I speak to you, it is the voice of God
> that sounds
> And all that I say is essential to you.
> I am the joyful telephone
> That transmits the songs and discourses of
> Heaven.

Louis had gradually stopped talking about his visions and revelations in front of his doctors. He obeyed the rules of the asylum and was treated well. He was allowed books – he loved reading history – and discussed religion and politics at local meetings of a group called *Le Cercle Catholique*. He made friends with the manager of the asylum, and even went on carriage jaunts with his family. Meanwhile, his own family was wild with anxiety at not hearing from him, for at first John Lee did not tell them where he was. Until July 1876, they had no idea what had happened to him. When they did find out, they were devastated.

In November of that year, Louis had a visitor from Red River. It was Archbishop Taché.

"Be my liberator," Riel begged him. "I want to reach the United States."

The archbishop believed he was better off where he was. But he did arrange for Louis to write to his family. By early 1877, letters began to fly back and forth. Careful letters, dealing only with family news and day-to-day life.

"I began this year with no way to send you New Year's greetings," he wrote to his mother. "But it's never too late to let the ones you love know how much good you wish for them." He inquired after the health of all the family, and sent his blessings. "Don't worry about me," he concluded. "I am under God's protection, and all will be well…"

By January 1878, Riel was well enough to be released. "Today I feel better," he told a doctor at the asylum. "I even laugh at the proud hallucinations of my brain. My mind is clear, but when one speaks of the Métis, of those poor people pursued by Orange fanaticism… Oh! Then my blood boils, my head swirls and…"

The doctor was watching him narrowly. "And?" he prompted.

"And it is better that I talk about something else," finished Louis, meeting his gaze with a smile.

To his old friend Dr. Lachapelle he wrote:

> I thank you for all the trouble you have taken to help me when I was unable to look after myself. I am extremely grateful for everything you did for me during the great trials to which it pleased God to subject me. My generous friend, Dr. Roy, told me, when I recovered, that you more than anyone else had taken the trouble to have me moved from Longue Pointe to Beauport. I thank you all the more because it was in the latter asylum that I had the good fortune to recover my senses. I was treated there as charitably as any lunatic could be.

Dr. Roy, the superintendent of Beauport, said that Riel was cured "more or less." Yet Louis's writings show that he never stopped believing in his mission as a prophet, and in his revelations about the Church of the Shining Mountains.

9

Wanderer

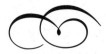

"Come for a good long visit," Father Barnabé had written Riel. "A year at least will do you good." So as soon as he left Beauport, Louis went straight to Keeseville. He dreamed of farming out west, possibly in Nebraska, but lacked funds. So he decided to farm near Keeseville instead, and the kind-hearted priest loaned him money to get started. Later that spring, Riel rented land and planted crops of corn and potatoes.

Soon after he arrived, he and Evelina Barnabé fell deeply in love. Again, Louis turned to poetry. Eagerly he wrote,

> If my joys suit you
> I hope that soon I can name you

Jean and Marie-Angélique, the children of Louis Riel. They were born during his stay in Montana and returned with their parents to Canada in 1884.

Gabriel Dumont. Known as "the Prince of the Prairies," he was the master military strategist of the Métis in the North-West.

Among those whom my heart knows how to love
And you will be one of those who belong to me

Louis spent a happy spring watching his crops sprout under the warm sun and strolling with Evelina on wooded paths beside the Au Sable River. The old lilac bush at the front of the Barnabé house burst into bloom, and its sweet scent wafting through the open windows inspired Riel to more dreams, more poems.

The lips of my beloved
Tempt my mouth more than watermelon
When I am thirsty. They are chaste and ruby,
Sweeter to taste than bees' nectar.
Her cheeks are the loveliest tint.
Their rose and white are like the blossoms of
the laurel,
More beautiful when they come and go
Especially under the influence of love.

There was a bench under the lilac – *their* bench, they called it – where he and Evelina often sat and talked. One day their hands touched, his brown, work-roughened fingers closing over her slender white ones.

Louis took a deep breath. "Evelina, *ma belle,...*" he began, but then he stopped. How could he ask her to marry him? He hadn't a penny and had just spent years in an asylum. What kind of future could he offer her?

But Evelina's eyes were shining. "Yes, Louis," she said, boldly answering his unasked question. "I will be your wife!"

He kissed her hand. "But I have nothing. We must wait…"

She nodded. "I know you will make a proper home for me someday. Until then, we must keep our engagement a secret. Fabien understands our love. But Maman…"

Louis sighed, remembering Marie-Julie Guernon's mother long ago. Must his love affairs always be conducted in secret? But he agreed.

∞

Riel's harvest was poor. By September he was in New York City looking for work, but nothing turned up. And old passions were kindling in him again. He met with a group of Fenians and tried unsuccessfully to interest them in backing a Métis republic. After that, Louis dropped in at Keeseville to say goodbye, then set off for St. Paul. He knew Bishop John Ireland planned to establish a Catholic colony in Minnesota, and he hoped to work for him. But though he had a pleasant interview he heard nothing more. He lingered in St. Paul until January, mulling over his plans for a republic and writing poems and love letters to Evelina. Then he went to stay with a friend near St. Joseph.

His mother, sisters, and brothers came to visit him. Seeing them again felt bittersweet. The "little ones" were all grown up. Octavie brought her husband, Louis Lavallée, and Eulalie was betrothed. Henriette was a slender young lady of seventeen. Joseph was courting one of the Marion girls, and Alexandre, his "little pet," was attending St. Boniface College. Where had the years gone? And Sara still toiled as a missionary at Île-à-la-Crosse. Would he ever see her again?

∞

On January 20, 1879, Riel went to meet Joseph Dubuc at the nearest railway station. Their eyes locked, and they shook hands formally. The thought of Dubuc sitting in his seat in Parliament still scorched Riel's proud soul. At a local hotel, they met with Ambroise Lépine, his brother Maxime, and other old friends. Bitterly, they discussed the wrongs of the Manitoba Métis.

"Oh, yes, there have been land grants," admitted Ambroise Lépine. "But the government put so many niggling regulations on them that a lot of us didn't get them."

"And new settlers grabbed much of the best land while the government delayed our claims," put in his brother.

"I hear many Métis are moving on to the Saskatchewan territory," said Riel.

Ambroise nodded. "Yes, and speculators buy up their Red River lands for a song."

Riel heard them out. "I think what has happened is an outrage," he said at last. "But what does anyone care about the opinions of a poor lunatic? I spent time in an asylum. It's useless to try to hide it."

"Your people don't think you're a lunatic," replied Dubuc.

Riel gave him a sharp glance.

"All your friends believe you never were mad," Dubuc went on. "They say either the government had you locked up for revenge, or you pretended to be mad."

Louis's eyes lit up. "What you say is true," he said. "I did pretend to be mad. I thought that a poor fool would be pitied. Then my enemies would cease persecuting my people. That's the explanation of the whole business." He spoke on for half an hour about how he had fooled everyone.

The others nodded approval, but Dubuc looked doubtful.

He doesn't believe me, thought Riel. "Anyway," he went on, I don't wish anyone to petition for a pardon for me."

"Why not?" asked Ambroise Lépine. "You could come home then." For he had chosen to serve out his jail sentence rather than accept exile.

"I am not a murderer. I have not committed any crime," replied Riel. "So I have no need of a pardon. And I don't care about a full amnesty, either. I want to stay here, on the frontier, a living and perpetual protest against England for its ill-intentioned proceedings against me."

Meanwhile, Father Barnabé wrote that Evelina was seriously ill. Riel wrote to her about his plans and sent verses to her. By spring, she was better. "I often go and sit under the lilacs, which are ready to bloom," she wrote. "I am carried back to the days when we were so happy, both of us seated on the same bench." But she fretted that she might not be fit for life in the West, and that she was "too humble" for the high position he might occupy if his plans for a new republic succeeded. Perhaps Louis worried that she might be right, that life in the West might be too hard for her. After May 1879, he stopped writing to her.

In August, Riel set off for the Saskatchewan territory. As he jolted westward in an ox cart, he was planning a new strategy. He now hoped to create a great confederacy of Métis and First Nations that would invade western Canada from a base in Montana. Then he planned to set up a provisional government and secure the rights of his people. As a first step, he went to Wood Mountain to meet with Sitting Bull, the famous Sioux chief. The scarred old warrior gazed at him impassively as he talked.

"I know how desperate the situation of the First Nations is," said Louis. "The buffalo are almost gone. Many Aboriginal Peoples face famine, even those who signed treaties with Canada."

"There is no one who does not know that," the chief replied.

"It is time to act. We must force Canada to recognize our rights in this land. If the Métis and the First Nations stand together we can do it!" Riel insisted.

After this meeting, Riel moved on south to a Métis camp near the Milk River in Montana. Over the winter, he contacted other First Nations, trying to win their support for his invasion scheme. But none would commit to a definite plan.

Meanwhile, Louis struggled to adapt to life in a Métis hunting camp. He was shocked by the drinking and violence created by the liquor trade. And, tenderfoot that he was, he found life in a drafty cabin in the bitter Montana winter apppalling. But in December he proudly wrote to his brother Joseph, "They have done me the honour of electing me *chef du camp.*" He took his new authority as the community leader seriously, and lectured the Métis men about their drinking and the violence it led to. Some turned against him, and he was even threatened with violence himself. In a poem, he wrote,

> One day you stuck your fist in my chest,
> Trying to frighten me. You made a row
> Because in camp, I put unbridled rebels like you
> In their place...

To keep body and soul together, Riel chopped wood, acted as translator, and did some small trading. In the spring of 1880, he moved south with a group of thirty to forty families of buffalo hunters. At Fort Benton he made a formal declaration that he wished to become an American citizen. Later that year, he got permission from the Army commander at the fort for his group to winter on a nearby reservation. The winter that followed was harsh, the worst in years. The embers of his life barely aglow, Louis stopped writing to his family. But nothing shook his devotion to the Métis people. "I am the only one who can lead them," he wrote.

Meanwhile, Louis saw a chance for a little personal happiness. He was thirty-seven years old now, and had still had no family of his own. In 1881, he began to court dark-eyed Marguerite Monet *dit*

Bellehumeur, a young Métisse. She was lovely and devoted to him, and marrying her would bind his life even more closely to the Métis people. He wrote,

> Her living faith and her uprightness
> Of spirit are good to see.
> Ah! What a fine creature she is
> She always does her duty.
> I have the benefit of knowing
> That her love isn't changeable
> When she loves, she loves completely.
> Her glance entices me.

But to his anger and embarrassment, many Métis in the camp found his late love affair uproariously funny. They mocked their prim-and-proper leader and made rough jokes about his romance. As always, he poured out his hurt in poetry:

> Every boy in the world
> Chooses his love.
> I too have a beloved
> That I see every day.
> But people gainsay
> My humble and good faith.
> In order to wrong me
> They speak evil of me…
>
> Ten painful years
> Have I laboured for my fellow-countrymen.
> They wish me to forego
> All allowable happiness,

Alas, and live
Joyless and friendless…

Louis and Marguerite married on April 27, 1881. No priest was available, so it was a "country" marriage. Riel fretted about this and wrote:

It is the long absence of a priest
My girl, that has forced us
To marry this way.
My girl, you will not be shamed.

A Jesuit priest performed a religious ceremony for them the next year, two months before their son, Jean, was born.

∞

In the autumn of 1881, Riel and Marguerite moved with the Métis band to Rocky Point on the Missouri River. Louis had received some money from the sale of land in Red River, so he set up a small business as a travelling trader. Still worried about the effects of the liquor trade on the Métis, he launched a lawsuit against a liquor trader named Simon Pepin. In the end, this cost him money he couldn't afford and he lost the case. An American named Alexander Botkin had helped him, so in the election of November 1882, Riel campaigned for Botkin and the Republican Party. Democratic Party politicians then falsely accused Riel of election fraud – encouraging Métis not qualified to vote to cast a ballot. He was clapped in jail. Louis was soon free on bail, but this lawsuit, too, cost him dear. However, all charges against him were finally dismissed.

Through all of this, amid the hubbub of Métis hunting camps, in dingy lodgings on his trading trips, Riel was writing a book. He called it the *Massinahican*, a Cree word that referred to the Bible. The *Massinahican* was to be the bible of his new religion. In it he summed up the revelations he had received from God. For now, though, he continued to worship in the traditional Catholic faith, sure that someday God would tell him the time was right to reveal his new religion.

∞

"You have a letter, Louis?" Marguerite asked one day in early 1883.

"It's from Sara," he told her. "And here's a greeting for you, her new sister-in-law."

Marguerite flushed with pleasure as he read her the loving message.

Louis sat down at once to reply. His eyes misted as he reread Sara's promise that God would yet reward his good intentions. She still believed in him! "Alone in the midst of a world that does not want my ideas, I am obliged to be silent and keep within myself my great hopes of God," he wrote. "God knows what price the kind words in your letter have in my eyes!"

But he did not share his next letter with Marguerite, for it was from Evelina, the girl he left behind him. After reading of Riel's marriage in a newspaper, she had tracked down a Montana address for him. In scathing words, she demanded that he tell her the truth about his marriage and accused him of destroying her happiness. Burning with indignation, Louis sat down and drafted a response. *She* had wanted a proper home before they married, he reminded her. *She* had expressed doubts about their love... It's not known whether he ever sent this reply, but to the end of his life he kept all of Evelina's letters.

∞

Times were hard for the little Riel family that spring. They had no money, and Marguerite was expecting another baby. Louis was upset by a strange vision he had of his father, and said he felt "a very strong moral sadness." In desperation, he took a job as a shepherd, while Marguerite worked as domestic help. Then Riel was offered a teaching position at St. Peter's Mission, near Sun River, Montana. At last he would be earning regular pay, and they would be able to settle down and educate their children at the mission school. The Riels arrived at St. Peter's in April and moved in with Joseph Swan, a Métis from Red River. But, "My wife and children and I, we have no home," Louis wrote. "We live with others. We have neither beds nor pillows. We sleep on straw."

In late June, Riel returned to Manitoba. His exile had long since expired, and he had become an American citizen. It was time for a visit – Henriette was getting married, and he also wanted to see to land claims there. His arrival was hot news in Winnipeg, and reporters from two newspapers hurried out to St. Vital to interview him. About the Red River Resistance and Scott's execution, he insisted, "I am more and more convinced every day, without a single exception, that I did right."

As friends and relatives gathered for the wedding celebrations, Louis wrote jokingly to Marguerite, "I have hardly been able to sleep on account of the large number of visitors." Yet not all his old friends welcomed him. He had a falling-out with Archbishop Taché, and his relationship with Joseph Dubuc and other prosperous French-speaking Manitobans felt strained, too. "No one wanted me in the influential political circles of Manitoba," he wrote, forlornly. "I am forgotten as if I were dead."

But not by everyone. At the wedding, Métis from the village of Batoche on the South Saskatchewan River sought him out.

"Our river lots are being threatened by new surveys," Napoléon Nault told him. "And English-speaking settlers are pouring in."

"We petitioned the government," added Damase Carrière, "but there was no reply."

They gazed at him hopefully. "Ah, the same old story," said Riel, stroking his beard. He had much to ponder on the long dusty ride back to Sun River.

Louis and Marguerite's daughter Marie-Angélique was born that autumn, and in November he began his teaching job. He was well liked, but teaching small children wore him down. "My health suffers from the fatiguing regularity of having to look after children from 6 in the morning until 8 at night, on Sunday as well as on the days of the week..." he complained. "I do not get enough rest."

And the year 1884 began badly. In January, Riel learned that Sara had died, and his sorrow plunged him into deep depression. In April and May, he had fearful dreams and heard the voice of God say he would spend thirty years in purgatory. Yet at other times, he felt strangely exhilarated. "The jug of my spirit has come uncorked," he wrote. He took it as a sign that his true mission was beginning at last and began writing down prayers and meditations. Then he received letters from the Saskatchewan territory. The Métis there were hoping for his help. They were going to send a delegation to him.

On June 4, the delegation arrived, weary and dusty. Summoned from Sunday mass, Riel shook hands with their leader.

"You are a man who has travelled far," he said. "I don't know you, but you seem to know me."

The man's deep-set eyes twinkled. Of course he knew *Monsieur le président*. Hadn't they met long ago at Fort Garry? But then he had been a lithe young hunter who had ridden hundreds of kilometres to offer his help. No wonder Riel didn't recognize the burly middle-aged fellow he had become. "Yes," he said. "And I think you may know the name of Gabriel Dumont."

Riel made the delegation wait a day for his answer, and then he agreed to go back with them. On June 10,

the little cavalcade set out for the Saskatchewan country. Louis had promised to help the Métis win their
rights. He mentioned, too, that he had claims of his
own to settle with Canada. Now, as the wagon jolted
across the rolling prairie, he dreamed of compensation
at last for his sufferings. And that was not all. If God
willed it, if the time was right... Visions of a Métis
republic in the North-West and his Church of the
Shining Mountains shimmered before his eyes like a
mirage.

Part Four
Wildfire

Riel after the North-West Rebellion,
as a prisoner in General Middleton's camp.

10

Uprising

I t was a hero's welcome. When Riel and the delegation arrived at Fish Creek, more than fifty Métis
wagons were waiting to greet them. Men on horse-
back surged around Riel's wagon, cheering and firing
a *feu de joie*. Women and children in wagons
applauded. Beaming, Louis swept off his hat,
acknowledging the cheers, the sun glinting on his
wavy chestnut hair. Marguerite proudly slipped her
hand into the crook of his elbow. Her husband was
well respected among the Métis of Montana. But this
– this was different!

The next day they were whisked off to Charles
Nolin's house, near the village of Batoche. Louis's
cousin had been among the Red River Métis who had

left Manitoba and started over in Saskatchewan. The family settled into his comfortable two-storey house, and people came and went, eager to greet the famous Riel. "I have been received with open arms by everybody," Louis wrote to his brother Joseph.

Louis Schmidt soon arrived from Prince Albert and offered to give up his job at the land office to come and help Riel. "Stay where you are," said Louis. "You can be of great help to our people there. And keep writing dispatches about the Métis movement to *Le Manitoba*. We need good publicity!"

Riel's first speech to the Métis radiated good feeling. "The Métis and English-speaking mixed-bloods must work together to gain their rights," he told them. And he repeated the message to a meeting of mixed-bloods. Next he was invited to address an English-speaking audience in Prince Albert. At first, Louis hesitated. There were many Ontarians in Prince Albert, among them people who had hounded him for the death of Thomas Scott. But in the end he agreed, and his speech was a glowing success.

"I do not wish to cause trouble or raise disturbance," he told them. "My intentions are peaceful." He spoke of their hardships and the indifference of the Canadian government. "Gentlemen, do not compromise any of your rights," he urged. "Do protest. React within the bonds of constitutional energy." Only one rabid Riel-hater interrupted him, and the man was thrown out of the meeting.

Riel wrote happily to his family in Manitoba, "Not long ago I was a humble schoolmaster on the far away banks of the Missouri, and here I am today in the ranks of the most popular public men in the Saskatchewan... What has brought all this about?... it is God."

∞

Though Louis believed that God was on his side, he soon found out that most of the local clergy were not. Father Alexis André, whose parish was at Prince Albert, distrusted him. And when Riel met with First Nations chiefs to discuss their desperate need for more rations from the government, Father André became ever more worried, for he feared Riel might incite an uprising.

In early August, Louis made a speech criticizing local priests. "Why do they not back me wholeheartedly?" he demanded. And many listeners murmured their agreement.

Soon afterward, he and Father André had a row.

"You priests lead the Métis to obey the government even though their rights are trampled on," he told the old priest. "But they are a chosen people, with a special destiny you do not understand."

Father André tugged his grizzled grey beard in annoyance. "Nonsense!" he said.

Riel's temper flared. "My task is not just political," he shouted. "I have a special and divine mission to fulfill. The old Catholic religion is going to change. The Holy Spirit has told me that!"

"You are a fanatic," snapped Father André. "Your ideas are heretical!"

"You are a coward and a man sold to the government," Riel shot back. Turning on his heel, he stomped out.

Riel and his supporters began working on a petition to the government. A draft of it was ready by October. The document demanded aid for First Nations, patents for lands already settled, and special land grants for Métis to extinguish their aboriginal title to the land, as had been done in Manitoba. Tariff reform and homestead regulations were also requested. The Saskatchewan district was to become a province with responsible government, vote by ballot, and control of natural resources. Riel had added a list of his own grievances. After discussion, the petition was sent to the Secretary of State on December 16.

Meanwhile, Riel's rift with the clergy had deepened. He and other Métis leaders had confronted Bishop Vidal Grandin of Prince Albert over the priests' lack of support.

"Your clergy do not attend our meetings," they told him. "Do they not care about our grievances?"

Despite this, Riel still attended mass regularly. But inwardly, he burned with religious exaltation. He began keeping a diary, in which he wrote down prayers and conversations with God. He also jotted notes urging himself to fast and live ever more simply, keeping to a plain diet and drinking a broth of bull's blood as a tonic.

One day, he and Louis Schmidt were invited to a Métis wedding. "Where are you going, Louis?" Schmidt asked afterward, as a bountiful feast was spread and the fiddles were being tuned for the dancing.

"Upstairs," said Riel. "To pray." He spent the entire night on his knees.

In November, Father Fourmond, the priest at St. Laurent, circulated a petition calling for a subsidy for a Catholic school in his parish. Riel was furious, because he knew this petition would anger Protestants. It did, and Riel was blamed. Much of his hard work to unify French-speaking and English-speaking settlers was undone.

His resentment against the clergy smouldered. Then, one day in December, he burst in on Father André and other priests who were in the midst of a retreat. "You do not support our movement," he accused. "Do you even care what happens to the Métis people?"

"From now on we will treat you as an enemy," warned Father André.

At this, Louis fell to his knees and wept. They led him to the altar, and he swore never to lead an uprising against the government.

Father André knew Riel hoped for compensation for the wrongs he felt he had suffered, and thought that if he got it he might be persuaded to leave Canada. So he set up a meeting between Riel and Andrew MacDowall, the local representative to the North-West Council. Riel said that the government owed him an indemnity of $100,000 for services rendered. He had governed Manitoba from the passing of the Manitoba Act in May 1870 until the arrival of Wolseley's troops in August. He had convinced the Métis to support the Manitoba government against the Fenians in 1871, and

had given up a sure seat in Parliament to Cartier in
1872. By refusing for years to grant him the amnesty
promised in 1870, the government had made it impossible for him to live and earn a living in his own country. In addition, he had never received the 240 acres
(593 hectares) of land he was entitled to under the
Manitoba Act.

"For all these wrongs, I am willing to accept a first
installment of $35,000," he told Father André and
MacDowall. He could not resist getting in a pun,
adding with a smile, "My name is Riel, and I want
mat*erial*!" Then he went on, "If I am satisfied with the
deal agreed upon, the Métis will be, too."

MacDowall took this to mean that Riel was offering to sell out his supporters for personal financial gain.
However, Napoléon Nault claimed that Riel and other
Métis had discussed the amount of the indemnity at a
meeting and hoped to use the money to purchase a
printing press for a Métis newspaper. But MacDowall's
report intensified Prime Minister Macdonald's dislike
and distrust of Riel, and encouraged him to discount
the seriousness of Métis grievances.

For more than a month, people waited for the government's response to their petition. In late January, the
government set up a Land Claims Commission to create a list of Saskatchewan Métis who might receive
land grants, as had been done in Manitoba. But when
Riel at last saw the telegram announcing this, he was
outraged. "There are no land claims for Métis who

received them in Manitoba," he protested. "Nor any mention of patents for land already occupied!"

And there was no word of any compensation for him.

On February 24, Riel stood up before a meeting in the church at Batoche after the telegram had been read out. "The government has robbed the people of the West of their land!" he cried. "It refuses to listen to their grievances!" Then he lowered his voice, and his tone became caressing. "My work here is done," he went on. "I helped draft your petition. Well, you have the government's answer. I can do you no more good, for the government will not treat with me. It's time for me to return to Montana."

"No! No!" Angry voices echoed off the rafters.

A very old Métis tottered to his feet. "If you leave, nephew, we will go with you," he vowed, and the rest shouted their agreement.

Louis waited for the uproar to die down, his gaze moving from one eager face to another. "But the consequences?" he asked softly.

"We will accept them!" answered the voices of his people.

"Then I will not leave you," promised Riel.

On March 1, he told another meeting that it was time to try new tactics. "Perhaps the Métis should bare their teeth," he told them, his dark eyes burning.

The next day, Riel went to see Father André. "The Canadian government has broken all the promises it made to the Métis people under the Manitoba Act," he reminded him. "It did not grant the full amnesty it promised, and most people did not get the lands they

were entitled to. Now the same thing is happening
here. We must establish a provisional government to
renegotiate our rights. I want your support."

"Never!" said the old priest.

On March 7, the Métis of St. Laurent received
more bad news. The Canadian government had
refused most of them title to the land they had claimed
for years. They would have to apply again and fulfill
conditions like any other homesteaders.

"Now is the time," Riel told them. "Let us form a
provisional government."

Charles Nolin, however, was afraid to go that far.
He proposed nine days of prayer and reflection before
taking any action, and Riel agreed. But on March 15,
Father Fourmond announced at mass that he would
not allow anyone who took part in an armed uprising to
take communion.

"How dare you refuse the sacrament to those who
would take up arms in defence of their most sacred
rights?" cried Louis.

In his diary that night he wrote, "Lord our
God...allow us to take the same position we did in '69
and to maintain it most gloriously...."

∞

On March 17 some Métis happened to meet Lawrence
Clarke, the chief factor of the Hudson's Bay Company
post at Fort Carlton. "What do you think the government will do about Métis land claims?" they asked him.

"The only answer you will get will be bullets,"
Clarke told them. "And I saw five hundred North West

Mounted Police on their way to capture your leaders, especially Riel."

This was untrue, but the Métis hurried to warn Riel.

"I can wait no longer," he told them. "The time has come now to rule this country or perish in the attempt."

On March 19, Riel and a party of armed horseman rode up to the church at Batoche. They had already seized arms and ammunition and taken prisoners. Riel now proposed to hold a meeting in the church.

"I protest!" cried Father Moulin.

"Listen to him!" jeered Riel. "He's a Protestant!" Then, in a solemn voice, "Old Rome is fallen!"

They rode on through wet snow to St. Laurent. There, Riel declared a provisional government. He called it the Exovedate, a made-up word based on Latin. It meant "those chosen from the flock." The Exovedate included Gabriel Dumont and other Métis activists. Riel himself did not join the council. He preferred the role of prophet.

For the next few days Riel tried to persuade the English-speaking mixed-bloods to support the Exovedate. But they wanted to remain neutral. Meanwhile, Gabriel Dumont set out with a party of Métis to commandeer supplies from a store in Duck Lake, a village west of Batoche. Superintendent Leif Crozier of the North West Mounted Police also sent a patrol to collect the supplies. At Duck Lake the two parties clashed. After a great deal of shoving and shouting and brandishing of weapons, the police patrol retreated to Fort Carlton.

Superintendent Crozier then set off for Duck Lake with a larger force of mounted troops and men in sleighs. They even took along a small cannon. Meanwhile, Riel had joined about three hundred armed Métis gathered at Duck Lake.

"The police are coming back," warned a scout. "More men. With arms, a cannon!"

"We'll ambush them on the Carlton trail," ordered Dumont.

But police scouts saw them, and both sides sent men forward to parley. Suddenly there was a scuffle – a man on the police side moved his horse forward, and a Cree interpreter, who was unarmed, grabbed at the policeman's rifle. The gun went off, and the interpreter fell dead. Then Crozier gave the order to fire, and Isidore Dumont, Gabriel's elder brother, was the first Métis to die.

As the Métis returned fire, Riel sat his horse in plain view, bullets whistling around him. He prayed aloud and held up a crucifix. After half an hour, the police retreated.

"After them!" ordered Dumont.

"No!" cried Riel. "There has been too much blood spilled already. Come, we must pray for the dead."

It was a thrilling victory. With only a few losses, the Métis had forced the famous North West Mounted Police to turn tail and run. Better yet, the police evacuated Fort Carlton that night and retreated to Prince Albert.

"Let me attack them in the dark," urged Dumont. "We can kill many that way."

Riel shook his head. "It's too savage," he replied.

The Métis "liberated" many valuable supplies from the Hudson's Bay store at the fort. And from papers left behind they learned that an armed force was already on its way from Canada. Prime Minister Macdonald had ordered General Middleton west on March 23. Canadian troops would be sent by train to the railhead at Fort Qu'Appelle, and from there they would march on Batoche.

After Duck Lake, Riel had no hope of support from white settlers, and the English-speaking mixed-bloods remained neutral. But he still hoped other Métis and the First Nations people would rally to his cause. The past summer, Big Bear and other chiefs had already asked him to help create a list of their grievances against the government. During the fall and winter, Dumont had also maintained his network of contacts with tribes along the North Saskatchewan River. So after Duck Lake, Riel sent more messages to these tribes and to the Métis of the Saskatchewan district. "Take provisions and ammunition," he wrote, "and come to us." But few Métis arrived, and the First Nations followed their own agenda. Some militant warriors were encouraged by the Métis victory. Against the advice of their senior chiefs, they decided to attack. There were raids at places such as Battleford, Lac La Biche, and Frog Lake. A number of people, including two priests, were killed and others were taken prisoner. Only a few Sioux and Cree warriors went to Batoche.

Riel hoped that the threat of a rising by the First Nations would force the Canadian government to negotiate. But newspapers in the East trumpeted the killings of priests and settlers, and Riel was blamed. The threat of an Indian war increased the number of volunteers eager to rush west on the Canadian Pacific

Railway and put down the Métis rebellion. Few asked what had driven desperate people to rebel in the first place.

∽

"If we don't do something Middleton will be on our doorstep," Dumont told Riel. For on April 6 the Métis had learned that Canadian troops were on their way from Fort Qu'Appelle.

"Reinforcements may soon join us," countered Riel. "We must wait and strike the enemy when they get closer."

"Why not harass them now? Keep them from sleeping at night. Demoralize them," urged Dumont. "That's the way to make them lose heart!"

"We must wait for our enemies to attack us," said Riel.

"But..." Dumont's words trailed away. He had confidence in Louis's faith and his prayers, and believed God would listen to him. They all did.

So Riel and the Exovedate focused on religious issues. Louis prayed and wrote down his revelations. Some of these he brought to the Exovedate, which voted on the measures he advised. Among these were changing the day of worship from Sunday to Saturday, and renaming the names of the days of the week. The council had already voted him prophet of the Métis.

But despite his trust in his revelations, even Riel had his moments of dread. On April 21, he wrote in his diary: "I have seen the giant – he is coming. It is Goliath."

At last, Dumont confronted Riel. "The men's nerves are in tatters from doing nothing," he complained. "We must act!"

"You know my thinking," replied Riel. "And the Exovedate backs me."

"But why give all the advantages to the enemy?" demanded Dumont. "Let me slow them down, give our allies time to arrive."

Riel gave in. "All right!" he sighed. "Do as you wish."

"We'll deal with them as we do buffalo!" growled Dumont.

On the night of April 23, Dumont rode to Fish Creek with a force of two hundred Métis. Riel went with him and insisted that they get down on their knees and pray at every stop. Word came that police were moving along the Qu'Appelle road, so Dumont sent twenty-five men and Riel back to guard Batoche. "We won't be saying the rosary so much now, so we'll move faster," he joked as he and his men rode on.

Dumont hid his men among the trees and bushes of the ravine. The next morning, Canadian scouts spotted Métis horsemen, and the chance of an ambush was lost. The Canadians moved forward, and firing began. Middleton had a force of eight hundred men and a nine-pounder cannon. But the Métis fought fiercely, falling back, as ordered, when they ran out of ammunition. By afternoon there were only fifty-four Métis fighters left in the ravine. In the nick of time, Dumont's brother Édouard galloped up with seventy reinforcements.

Back in Batoche, Riel had gathered the women and children around him. The shooting and cannon fire at Fish Creek could be clearly heard. Kneeling on the ground, his arms extended in the form of a cross, Louis stormed heaven. "Hear my prayers, O Lord!" he cried.

As darkness fell, the shooting died away and both forces fell back. Against all odds, the Métis had fought Middleton's troops to a standstill. In the East, the battle was reported as a stinging defeat for the Canadian forces. At Batoche, the Métis celebrated their miracle.

∽

Middleton waited for reinforcements before he advanced again. Dumont spent the time having trenches and rifle pits dug around the village. When the Battle of Batoche began, on May 9, he rushed his men from one position to another, making his force seem far larger than it really was. The Canadian troops had better weapons – modern rifles, cannon, and even a Gatling gun, a kind of early machine-gun. But although they skirmished with the Métis fighters, they failed to capture the village.

Amid the whine of bullets, the boom of cannon, and the deadly chatter of the Gatling gun, Louis walked around holding a crucifix. He read from the Bible and prayed that the enemies of the Métis would be destroyed. But on the morning of May 12, the Canadian troops, weary of Middleton's cautious tactics, stormed the village.

As the rifle pits were overrun, Riel knelt in prayer. "Work your miracle now," urged one of his followers. "It's time!" But this time there was no miracle. The Métis fought house by house, but at last the surviving fighters retreated, still firing. They faded into the woods, and the battle was over.

∞

Riel and Dumont met among the trees.

"What are we going to do?" asked Riel.

Dumont shrugged. "We are beaten. We must die," he said. "You must have known that in taking up arms we would be defeated. Very well, they must destroy us."

Marguerite Riel and the children were hiding in a cave near the river. Dumont found blankets for them, and Riel later saw them safely across the river to the house of Moïse Ouellette. Then he returned to the other shore. In the confusion, he and Dumont missed each other, and Dumont was told that Riel had surrendered. On May 13, when he received a letter from Middleton offering protection, Gabriel responded bluntly, "You tell Middleton that I am in the woods, and that I still have ninety cartridges to use on his men." Soon after, he rode for the Montana border.

Riel's courage was of a different sort. Let them put me on trial, where I can plead for the Métis cause, he told himself. Let the people of Canada hear what I have to say. I will surrender. "I'm the one they want," he told Napoléon Nault, "and when my enemies have me they'll be overjoyed: but my people will be at peace and they will get justice." To Middleton, Louis wrote: "My council are dispersed. I wish you would let them [be] quiet and free... Would I go to Batoche, who is going to receive me? I will go to fulfill God's will."

Later that day, with a white handkerchief tied around his sleeve and Middleton's letter in his pocket, he walked up to a party of Canadian scouts.

"Who goes there?" came the challenge.

"Louis Riel," was the reply.

11

Trials

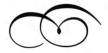

O n July 29, 1885, the heat in the tiny courtroom in Regina was stifling. Sitting in the prisoner's dock, Riel gazed at the crowd that packed the room. Reporters, soldiers, police, lawyers, and the curious had come to see him tried for the crime of high treason against the Queen. There was even a bevy of ladies, the starched frills of their summer dresses wilting in the heat. They fanned themselves and whispered about the "bloodthirsty rebel."

Louis fought down his disappointment. He had wanted to be tried before the Supreme Court of Canada, not in this dingy place! But now the next witness was called. It was Charles Nolin, and Riel burned with indignation as he listened to his cousin's

Riel addressing the court in Regina during his trial in July 1885.
His requests to share in the questioning of witnesses were refused.

testimony. Nolin accused him of planning to destroy Manitoba and the North-West. And his own defence team wasn't asking the proper questions of this witness – or of any other witness! They only wanted to prove that he was not guilty because he was insane. If they won, he might be locked up in an asylum for life. His soul shuddered at the thought.

At last Louis could bear it no longer. He stood up and begged the judge to let him say a few words. "My counsel come from Quebec, from a far province," he said. "They have to put questions to men with whom they are not acquainted, on circumstances they don't know…"

"You will be able to address the jury later in the trial, Mr. Riel," said the judge.

"But the witnesses are passing, and the opportunities!" Louis protested. "Already I have two hundred questions not asked by my counsel!"

"Your honour, we must resign if Mr. Riel interferes," said one of his lawyers.

"I wish to retain my lawyers. But I cannot abandon my dignity!" pleaded Riel. "Here I have to defend myself against the accusation of high treason, or I have to consent to the animal life of an asylum. I don't care much about animal life if I am not allowed to carry with it the moral existence of an intellectual being."

On the following days, Riel listened as lawyers for the Crown tried to prove that he was completely sane, that he had offered to desert the Métis for a bribe of thirty-five thousand dollars, that his vanity and ambition alone had caused the uprising. Then Riel's lawyers called witnesses. Father André and Father Fourmond said Riel was "completely a fool" on questions of religion and politics, that when contradicted, he would fly into a temper, and "use violent expressions." Dr. François Roy, from the Beauport asylum, testified that Louis had suffered from "megalomania."

At last, on July 31, Riel was allowed to address the jury. "I feel blessed by God for all those who testified that I am not mad," he began. Then he tried to explain Métis grievances. "The rebellion would have remained constitutional if we had not been attacked," he said. As to his religious ideas, "I wished to leave Rome aside because it divided Catholics and Protestants," he told the court. And he claimed to be the prophet of the New World. As to politics, he concluded, "I am simply a guest of the Half-breeds of the Saskatchewan. I worked to better the condition of the people of the Saskatchewan at the risk of my life. I have never had any pay. It has always been my hope to have a fair living one day. It will be for you to pronounce – if you say I was right, you can conscientiously acquit me, as I hope through the help of God you will."

His speech was a reasonable explanation of his actions. It undermined his lawyers' argument that he was insane, and made it clear that he did not want to be acquitted on those terms.

The next day, the judge addressed the jury. Then Louis knelt as the jury withdrew to deliberate. After only an hour, they returned.

"We find the defendant guilty," said the foreman. "But we wish to recommend clemency."

Once again, Riel was allowed to speak. He first thanked the jury. "Should I be executed... I would not be executed as an insane man," he said. Then for three hours, while his audience sweated and fidgeted in the sweltering heat, Louis talked about his "fifteen years' war," his long struggle for his people against the government of Canada. Overcome by emotion, he sometimes rambled, and paused to collect himself. He described the Red River Resistance, and his pride at being the father of the Province of Manitoba. He spoke of his mission as the prophet of the New World, and of his vision of people from many lands, not just Ontario, pouring into the North-West to populate it.

"Is that so insane?" he asked.

He mentioned land rights for the Métis and Indians. "We are not birds," he said. "We have to walk upon the ground..."

At last he stopped, exhausted.

The judge read the sentence, the words dropping like stones into the silence of the courtroom. "Louis Riel," he said, "on the 18th of September next you will be taken to the place appointed for your execution and there be hanged by the neck until you are dead. And may God have mercy on your soul."

Locked in a small cell in the Regina North West Mounted Police barracks, Riel felt death creep closer day by day. "How has death become my fiancée, with the horror that I feel for her?" he wrote in his diary. "How can she follow me with an attention equal to the repulsion she inspires in me?"

Yet one small flame lived among the ashes of his hopes. The newspapers told him of the storm of public opinion in his favour in Quebec. Many people there believed he was a francophone scapegoat – that the government of Canada wished to hang him because he was not English. The arguments of Riel's lawyers and his history as an inmate in asylums had convinced the Quebec public that he was also insane and should not be executed. In public meetings and in their newspapers, French Canadians were putting pressure on the government of Canada not to execute Riel. Old friends like Masson, Fiset, and Desjardins had organized the committee that had paid his legal expenses. Now they did their best to save him. Of course, in Ontario the tide of opinion ran the other way, and many clamoured for his death. Meanwhile, his lawyers appealed his case to the Court of Queen's Bench in Manitoba. If that failed, they would appeal directly to the Lords of the Privy Council in London.

Now, in the shadow of death, there was another appeal that Riel had to make. "What must I do to be reconciled with the Church?" he asked Father Fourmond.

"You must sign a document abjuring your heresies and affirming your faith in the Catholic Church," the priest told him. "And you must read it aloud before the other Métis imprisoned here."

"Prepare the document, Father, and I will sign it," said Louis. "I cannot be without the comfort of the Church now."

But he sometimes still spoke of himself as a prophet and was eager to share his revelations from the Holy Spirit.

"I saw the spirit of Bishop Bourget as a blazing sun," he told Father André one day in August.

"You must control these foolish and extravagant thoughts," Father André told him. "You have given up your heresies, remember."

"My ideas are like bubbles coming to the surface in a pan of hot water," Louis protested. "I will renounce them if you don't approve. But I can't help having them!"

In the end, the priests agreed to let him be as long as he said nothing contrary to the teachings of the Church.

∞

Marguerite and the children were staying with his mother at St. Vital. "You may well believe," Riel wrote to his wife, "that I am concerned about your health and about our dear little children. Be brave and offer your tears to the Holy Virgin and Our Lord."

He also wrote letters to the American consul at Winnipeg, and later sent a plea to the president of the United States. He reminded Grover Cleveland that he had become an American citizen and asked for help on that basis. And many Americans in the northeastern states remembered him. They wrote letters and telegrams to the Canadian government on his behalf. So did people in cities like Chicago and St. Paul. But the American government did not act.

As the date of his execution drew nearer, Louis wrote a meditation in which he said,

Death has gained a day on me since
yesterday.
Death is busy taking away my tomorrow.
She carries it off as swiftly as the pendulum
of the clock counts the seconds.
My God! Help me to prepare myself.

Late one evening, Corporal Tabor, the youngest of
his guards, let himself into Riel's cell. Louis noticed
that he seemed ill at ease.

"From now on a guard must be in your cell twenty-
four hours a day, Mr. Riel," Tabor explained. "Until..."

"Until my execution?"

Tabor nodded. "The death watch. It's the rule."

"So we must see a lot of each other," said Riel.
Then, "Mr. Tabor, do you happen to play cribbage?"

Tabor nodded. So after that they played to pass
the time whenever Tabor was on duty.

In early September, Julie, Marguerite, and Joseph
Riel were allowed to visit.

"I wanted to come before, Louis," cried
Marguerite. "But..."

"Hush. I know," he told her. For she was expecting a baby and was in poor health. "Now I want all of
you to remember that there is still hope. If it is God's
will I shall be saved."

On September 17, the day before the scheduled
execution, the officer in charge came to Riel's cell.
"You have been granted a month's reprieve while the
appeal process goes on," he told him.

Overwrought, Louis burst into tears. Then, mas-
tering himself, he sat down and wrote to his mother, "I

have twenty-nine more days to prepare myself for death and to enjoy life." But now he began to worry again about the poverty of Marguerite and the children. He thought of having a photographer take pictures of him, which could be sold to give them a small income, but nothing came of this.

He had visits from Father André every day. "Perhaps you would like another confessor," Louis's former enemy said. "I can ask to be relieved of this duty."

But Louis had softened toward the crusty old man. "No, Father!" he replied. "I want only you."

He and Tabor kept up their cribbage games, and he had become friendly with other guards too, even writing snippets of verse for them:

> Duncan McDonell
> I do
> Wish you
> Well.

> O my fair guard Frederick Rhodes
> You wish me to write you a line
> Remember that there are two roads
> One is bad, the other divine
> If you know how to make your choice
> You will have a future of joyce.

And he noted,

> After a while, I know the Boys
> Will gather all my little scrips;
> Publish them as one of their joyce

And as a tie of our friendships!
To celebrate
A true Prophet: Louis "D" Riel.

Throughout October, Louis wrote down more and more prophecies and revelations from the Holy Spirit. Swedes, Norwegians, and Danes would hear the prophet of the New World, he predicted. He foresaw devastating wars and the alliance of Britain and the United States. He also set about renaming the universe. "God wants the Big Dipper to be called the 'Fabien Barnabé,' he wrote. "God wants the North Star to be named 'Henriette.'"

His execution was postponed once again to give his lawyer time to reach England and petition the Privy Council. But there, permission to appeal Riel's case was denied, and the execution was rescheduled for November 10. Riel's nerves quivered at each postponement, but the flame of his hope burned a little higher. For he read in the newspapers that in Quebec the public outcry over his sentence was reaching a climax. Might the government not spare him after all?

News came that Marguerite had given birth to their third child, a son, on October 21. But the baby had lived for only two hours. In a letter to Henriette, Riel poured out his grief. "The misery that I feel in seeing my little one taken from me without ever being able to embrace him without ever being able to give him my love strikes to the innermost depths of my soul," he wrote.

∽

In early November, Riel's execution was postponed yet again, to November 16. Soon after, three men, one after another, visited Louis. He already knew Dr. Jukes, the staff surgeon of the Mounted Police. The other two told him they were reporters. But they were not. The uproar in Quebec over Riel's sentence had convinced Prime Minister Macdonald that doctors must decide whether Riel now knew right from wrong. If he did not, he could not be executed. But Macdonald knew that if he pardoned Riel, Ontario would turn against the Conservative party. If he did not, the Conservatives were finished in Quebec.

Dr. Jukes found Riel normal, "except upon certain religious and private matters (re Divine mysteries)." He liked him, and wrote that he wished "justice and popular clamour could be satisfied without depriving this man of his life." Later he had second thoughts, and sent a telegram to the government saying that the matter should not be decided without examining Riel's writings.

Dr. M. Lavell was the first "reporter" to interview Riel. He found him intelligent, and particularly noted his voice, "soft, mellow and sweet, interesting to a degree, drawing out the sympathies of the listener."

"I'm worried about my children," Louis told him, "that the disgrace of my being executed as a criminal may cause them to suffer."

Lavell found Riel to be sane, and feared that his testimony might help send him to the gallows.

Dr. F.X. Valade, the second "reporter," wrote to Lieutenant-Governor Dewdney of the North-West Territories,

> After having examined carefully Riel in private conversation with him and by testimony of persons who take care of him, I have come to the conclusion that he is not an accountable being, that he is unable to distinguish between wrong and right on political and religious subjects, which I consider well-marked typical forms of insanity under which he undoubtedly suffers, but on other points I believe him to be sensible and can distinguish right from wrong.

Dewdney telegraphed the text of the reports by Lavell and Valade to the prime minister, who prepared a memo based on them for the Cabinet. Despite Valade's point that Riel could *not* distinguish between wrong and right on political and religious subjects, the Cabinet decided that the execution must proceed.

J.A. Chapleau, who had been Riel's schoolmate at the Collège de Montreal, threatened to resign from the Cabinet over the issue. But in the end, none of the French-Canadian ministers resigned. "He shall hang," vowed Prime Minister Macdonald, "though every dog in Quebec bark in his favour." And in the report that was later presented to Parliament, Valade's crucial words were omitted.

∞

Riel had already written his will, leaving his love and his blessings to his family, and begging their forgiveness for the suffering he had caused them. He prepared himself to face death, but he still felt a flicker of hope. He had been spared so often before!

But on the evening of November 15, Colonel Irvine came to his cell. "I regret to inform you that the execution will be carried out at eight o'clock tomorrow morning," he announced.

Louis drew a ragged breath. "Ah. I thought I still had twenty-four hours," he replied. Now he could hear the sound of hammering through the thin walls of his cell. They were building the scaffold.

Riel ate a last meal of eggs and milk. As a memento of their companionship, he gave Corporal Tabor the cribbage board. Then he spent the night awake, praying with Father André. Henriette had sent him a rosary and a little vial of holy water from the shrine of Lourdes, in France, and he kept them close. After midnight, he wrote his last letters, and his children were much in his thoughts. He wrote to Marguerite, confiding them to her care and adding a tender postscript:

> I write a word of kindness according to God
> to my little, little Jean; a word of kindness
> and tenderness also to my little, little Marie-
> Angélique.
> Be brave. I bless you.

His last letter was to his mother, and in it he bade farewell to all.

> I embrace you all with the greatest affection.
> You, dear mother, I embrace as must a son
> whose soul is full of filial love.

You, my dear wife, I embrace as a Christian husband according to the Catholic spirit of conjugal union.

My dear little children, I embrace you as a Christian father should, blessing you to the full extent of divine mercy, for the present life and the life to come.

You my dear brother and sisters, brothers- and sisters-in law, nephews and nieces, close relatives and friends, I embrace you all with all the warmth of which my heart is capable. May you be happy.

Dear Mother,

I am your affectionate, submissive and obedient son

Louis "David" Riel

At five in the morning, Father André said mass for Riel, and at seven, he administered the sacrament of extreme unction. Louis then bathed, and old, worn clothes were handed him – a black coat, tweed trousers, a wool shirt, and moccasins.

"So shabby!" he said, with a reproachful glance. But he put them on.

At eight o'clock it was time. Sheriff Chapleau, a French Canadian, was supposed to march Riel to the scaffold, but he refused the duty. Deputy Sheriff Gibson went to fetch Louis instead, but on the threshold of the cell he stopped, unable to speak.

Riel looked up, pale but calm. "You want me, Mr. Gibson?" he asked. "I am ready."

Down the long corridor he padded in his moccasins, and into the guardhouse. There he knelt and
kissed the ivory crucifix he carried, while Father André
absolved him of his sins. Then Father McWilliams,
another priest, preceded him up the ladder that led to
the scaffold outside.

The morning was bright and cold, the sky infinitely
blue, the prairie glazed with sparkling frost. Riel took a
deep breath of the crisp air. His eyes searched the faces
of the small knot of witnesses gathered at the foot of the
scaffold to watch him die, and his lips parted. It was his
last platform, his last audience, his last chance. Surely
now the right words would come, glorious words that
would convince people of his sincerity, of his mission.
But he had promised Father André not to speak. He
glanced at the old priest, but Father André shook his
head. And Louis obeyed. There would be no last words.

The hangman stepped forward and bound Riel's
hands behind him. His face was solemn, but his eyes
gleamed in anticipation. For he had asked for this duty.
He had been a friend of Thomas Scott and one of Riel's
prisoners at Red River in 1870.

In the last moments, Father André broke down
and sobbed.

"*Courage, bon courage, mon père,*" Riel said softly.
Then the hangman slipped the mask and noose over his
head. There was sudden darkness, and Louis felt the stifling pressure of canvas against his nostrils as he inhaled,
the weight of the heavy knot behind his left ear...

The hangman leaned closer. "Louis Riel, you had
me once and I got away from you," he said. "I have you
now and you'll not get away from me!"

But perhaps Riel did not hear him, for as Father André wept he was reciting the Lord's Prayer with Father McWilliams. "...Lead us not into temptation, but deliver us from evil – "

The trap door sprang open beneath Louis's feet, and the world fell away.

Epilogue

The Legacy

Louis Riel devoted his life to the Métis cause. A fiery activist, he chose the side of the underdog and struggled against injustice as he saw it. Today, he is the subject of books, plays, poems, statues, and an opera, and his complete collected writings have been published in French and English. Many Canadians who know little about history or the Métis cause have heard of him.

There are a thousand "what ifs" in Louis's story. What if he had not allowed the execution of Thomas Scott? With his talents, and without the fanatical persecution of Ontario's Orange Protestants, he would surely have made a career in Canadian politics and held an honoured place as the "Father of Manitoba."

Statue of Louis Riel near the Manitoba Legislature.
He brandishes a roll of Métis rights that he fought so hard to win.

What if Lieutenant-Governor Archibald had reached Red River before Wolseley and his troops? There would have been a dignified handing-over ceremony with a *feu de joie*, and with the new lieutenant-governor in charge, Riel might never have had to flee at all.

What if the longed-for amnesty had come sooner, as had been promised? Riel would have been spared years of exile, and might never have experienced the religious revelations sparked by his suffering. Canada might have gained a politician and lost a prophet. In the North-West Rebellion of 1885, what if Riel had allowed Gabriel Dumont to fight an effective guerrilla war against the Canadian forces? The Métis were masters of the countryside, and had many links with other Aboriginal Peoples. They might have held out longer, and the Canadian government might have come to terms with them. Then there would have been no trial, no gibbet, and, of course, no martyr.

But it was Riel's fate to be an outlaw. His political hopes dashed, he plunged into a spiritual and emotional crisis that led to a vocation as a visionary and prophet. In some aboriginal cultures such a personal upheaval was believed to indicate the emergence of a shaman, a person whose spiritual vocation serves the people. For this reason, the emerging shaman was supported by the community and often found guidance from a mentor. But Louis had to face his crisis without such support. Fusing his visions and prophesies with the Catholic faith, he tried to forge a new religion to express the political and spiritual destiny of his people, the Métis.

Riel's Catholic, Apostolic, and Vital Church of the Shining Mountains did not survive him. But other nineteenth-century religious reformers, like Joseph Smith, had better luck. Today Smith's Church of Jesus Christ of the Latter Day Saints – the Mormon faith – is one of the world's fastest-growing religions. Was Riel necessarily less inspired than Smith? Like him, Louis wanted to found a new faith joining elements of the Old World with the New. Because he failed does not make his religious visions any less remarkable than those of one who succeeded.

Riel's life and especially his death shook the fault lines of Canadian society. His fate contributed to tensions between francophones and anglophones and the struggle between Quebec and Ontario. Many Québécois believed at the time – and some still believe – that Riel was executed not so much for leading a rebellion as for being a French and Catholic opponent of the Canadian government. That belief has had long-lasting consequences. The Parti national, Quebec's first truly nationalist party and a forerunner of today's Parti Québécois, was formed by Henri Mercier, a Riel supporter, as a direct response to his execution. Riel was also a pioneer in the field of aboriginal rights and land claims, and he has his place in histories that express the alienation of the West from the rest of Canada. Some western historians see Riel as the victim of capitalism – of eastern Canada's plan to exploit and develop the West purely for its own benefit.

In 1992, the House of Commons declared Riel to be one of the founders of Manitoba. Today, on November 16, the anniversary of his execution, Louis

Riel Day is celebrated in communities across Canada. Over the years, many people have also urged that he should be pardoned posthumously. But, pardon or no pardon, he is without doubt the last thing he would ever have expected to be – a genuine Canadian hero.

Louis Riel in Montana, around 1883. Even living as he did at times in rough hunting camps, he kept his dapper appearance.

Chronology of
Louis Riel
(1844–1885)

Compiled by Rhonda Bailey

LOUIS RIEL AND THE MÉTIS	CANADA AND THE WORLD
	1670 King Charles II of Britain grants a royal charter to the Hudson's Bay Company (HBC) for exclusive trading rights in Rupert's Land, the drainage basin of Hudson Bay. The charter territory includes most of what is today the Prairie provinces and northern Ontario.
1780 Marie-Anne Gaboury (maternal grandmother of Louis Riel) is born in Maskinongé, diocese of Trois-Rivières, Quebec.	
	1783 The Treaty of Paris formally recognizes the United States of America (U.S.)

LOUIS RIEL AND THE MÉTIS	CANADA AND THE WORLD
	Colonists loyal to the British Crown (Loyalists) leave the U.S. and move north into the Niagara Peninsula, Quebec, and Nova Scotia.
	The North West Company (NWC) is formed by a group of merchants in Montreal to manage the fur trade in the British territory to the west and north.
	1791 The British Constitutional (Canada) Act creates Upper Canada and Lower Canada, the future provinces of Ontario and Quebec.
	1803 The U.S. negotiates the purchase of the vast Louisiana Territory from the French.
1806 In Maskinongé, Marie-Anne Gaboury marries a fur-trader from Rupert's Land, Jean-Baptiste Lagimodière, formerly of Maskinongé. They are the future maternal grandparents of Louis Riel.	**1806** In the U.S., the Lewis and Clark Expedition reaches the Pacific Ocean.
Immediately following their marriage, the Lagimodières travel west by canoe. The journey ends at a Métis encampment on the Pembina River.	United Sates Army Lieutenant Zebulon Pike begins his explorations of the American west. After a Dutch surrender, the Cape Colony in southern Africa becomes a British colony.
1807 Marie-Anne Lagimodière gives birth to a baby girl. The Lagimodières travel to the HBC post	**1807** David Thompson of the NWC crosses the Rocky Mountains and establishes Kootenai House, the

LOUIS RIEL AND THE MÉTIS

Cumberland House, where Marie-Anne and her daughter are the first white females resident in the West.

The Lagimodières are in the North Saskatchewan region from 1807–1811. Marie-Anne accompanies her fur-trader husband on his hunting expeditions.

1811

Scots and Irish workmen, sent to prepare for the arrival of the first group of Selkirk's colonists, are transported to Churchill by HBC ships and dropped off. Led by Miles Macdonell, first governor of Assiniboia, they arrive at Red River the following summer.

1812

In the spring, Jean-Baptiste Lagimodière returns to Red River to settle with his family. He continues to hunt and is hired several times to supply food for the Selkirk settlers between 1812 and 1815.

CANADA AND THE WORLD

first fur-trading post in what is now southeastern British Columbia.

In the U.S., Robert Fulton's steamboat travels from New York to Albany on the Hudson River and inaugurates the world's first commercial steamboat service.

The British Slave Trade Act outlaws the slave trade within the British Empire.

1811

Thomas Douglas, the Earl of Selkirk, (Lord Selkirk) gains control of the HBC and arranges for a grant of 300,440 square kilometres of HBC land at Red River. Selkirk names the area Assiniboia and plans to establish an agricultural colony.

David Thompson crosses the Rocky Mountains through Athabasca Pass and journeys down the Columbia River to the Pacific.

Hand craftsmen called "Luddites" destroy machinery in English textile factories.

1812

British general Isaac Brock is killed at the Battle of Queenston Heights and becomes a Canadian hero.

Napoleon of France invades Russia.

LOUIS RIEL AND THE MÉTIS

The second group of Selkirk's colonists, from Ireland and the Hebrides, arrives at Red River in October. Houses are not ready and food is in short supply.

1814
Another group of Selkirk's colonists arrives at Red River. They are from Kildonan in the Scottish Highlands.

To ensure sufficient food for the settlers, Miles Macdonell forbids the export of any provisions from Assiniboia. This "Pemmican Proclamation" threatens the livelihood of the Métis.

1815
In the spring, the Métis, at the instigation of the NWC, harass the colonists until they force abandonment of the Selkirk colony.

During the summer, some settlers return, and new colonists arrive with Robert Semple, who has been appointed governor of the HBC territories.

Jean-Baptiste Lagimodière is employed to carry dispatches to Lord Selkirk in Montreal. He completes the 2900-kilometre journey on foot, during the winter.

Jean-Baptiste Riel, a NWC voyageur from Quebec, marries Marguerite Boucher, a Franco-Chipewyan

CANADA AND THE WORLD

1814
The Treaty of Ghent officially ends the War of 1812 in North America.

There is bitter rivalry between the NWC and HBC in British North America, as both fur trade companies try to control the trade.

The first steam locomotive is built, by George Stephenson in Great Britain.

1815
John A. Macdonald, the future first prime minister of Canada, is born.

Otto von Bismarck, future Prussian/German leader is born.

In Europe, Napoleon is defeated at the Battle of Waterloo and exiled.

LOUIS RIEL AND THE MÉTIS	CANADA AND THE WORLD

Métisse, at Île-à-la-Crosse in the North Saskatchewan region.

1816
At Seven Oaks, in a confrontation with a band of Métis led by Cuthbert Grant, twenty men from the HBC post Fort Douglas are killed, including Robert Semple. Only one of the Métis men is killed.

For his services to Lord Selkirk, Jean-Baptiste Lagimodière receives a grant of land between the east bank of the Red River and the Seine in the Red River Settlement. He builds a house there for his expanding family.

1817
Jean-Louis Riel (future father of Louis Riel) is born at Île-à-la-Crosse to Jean-Baptiste and Marguerite Riel.

1821
The Métis people have come to identify themselves as a nation, with aboriginal rights to the land.

1822
The Riel family returns from the West to Lower Canada, where young Jean-Louis Riel attends school and learns the trade of carding wool.

1816
An economic crisis in Britain causes large-scale emigration to Canada and the U.S.

1817
Riots against low wages take place in Derbyshire, England.

1821
After years of rivalry, the HBC and NWC are merged under the Hudson's Bay Company name. The British government extends the HBC's trade monopoly beyond Rupert's Land to include the territory of the North-West.

LOUIS RIEL AND THE MÉTIS

Julie Lagimodière (future mother of Louis Riel) is born to Jean-Baptiste and Marie-Anne Lagimodière in the Red River Settlement.

CANADA AND THE WORLD

1824
The Geological Survey of Canada is founded.

The Lachine Canal bypassing the rapids at Montreal is completed.

1834
Lord Selkirk's estate sells Assiniboia back to the HBC.

1834
York is incorporated as the city of Toronto. William Lyon Mackenzie is elected mayor.

1837
Gabriel Dumont, future Métis leader and Louis Riel's military commander during the North-West Rebellion, is born in the Red River Settlement.

1837
Rebellions occur in Upper and Lower Canada; the leaders – Louis-Joseph Papineau in Lower Canada and William Lyon Mackenzie in Upper Canada – go into exile in the U.S.

Victoria is crowned Queen of Great Britain and the Empire.

1838
Jean-Louis Riel comes back to Rupert's Land and works for the HBC.

1838
In Great Britain, Charles Dickens publishes *Nicholas Nickleby* and *Oliver Twist*.

Thousands of eastern Native Americans are removed from their ancestral homelands by the U.S. army and forced to move west. Many die along the way.

LOUIS RIEL AND THE MÉTIS

1840
A great buffalo hunt lasts two months. In the largest expedition ever to leave Red River, 1630 Métis people, including women and nearly 400 children, depart for the hunting grounds.

1842
Jean-Louis Riel goes to Canada East and enters a religious order. After a short time he withdraws because he feels he lacks a vocation for the priesthood.

1843
Jean-Louis Riel returns to the North-West and settles in St. Boniface on a river lot near that of Jean-Baptiste Lagimodière.

1844
Jean-Louis Riel marries Julie Lagimodière on January 21.

A son, Louis Riel, is born to Jean-Louis and Julie on October 22 in the Red River Settlement, Rupert's Land.

1845
Alexandre-Antonin Taché becomes an Oblate priest and a Catholic missionary in Rupert's Land.

CANADA AND THE WORLD

1840
The Act of Union is passed. Upper and Lower Canada will become Canada West and Canada East and unite to form the Province of Canada.

New Zealand becomes a British colony. By the Treaty of Waitangi the Maori cede sovereignty but not land.

1842
In Africa, the Boers set up the Orange Free State.

1843
In New Zealand, Maori revolts against Great Britain take place when settlers take Maori land, and the Maori retaliate by attacking the settlements.

1844
In the U.S., inventor Samuel Morse uses the first intercity electromagnetic telegraph line to send a message between Washington and Baltimore.

1845
Having been pardoned the year before, Louis-Joseph Papineau returns to Canada East.

LOUIS RIEL AND THE MÉTIS

CANADA AND THE WORLD

In Ireland, the potato famine begins. Hundreds of thousands of destitute Irish people emigrate to North America.

1846
At Île-à-la-Crosse, Father Taché establishes the first Roman Catholic mission in the Saskatchewan territory.

1846
The Oregon Treaty sets the forty-ninth parallel as the boundary between the United States and the British lands to the north. The British retain Vancouver Island.

1847
The census lists 4,871 inhabitants of the Red River colony; 50 per cent are Catholics.

1847
Egerton Ryerson produces a study of Native education that will become the model for future residential schools in Canada.

In the U.S., Mormons led by Brigham Young trek across country to escape religious persecution and establish Salt Lake City in Utah.

1848
A daughter, Sara, is born to Jean-Louis and Julie Riel.

1848
A group of radical young francophone intellectuals found the Parti rouge in Quebec.

The California Gold Rush begins.

Karl Marx and Friedrich Engels issue the *Communist Manifesto*.

1849
Jean-Louis Riel leads the Métis community of Red River to aid Pierre-Guillaume Sayer, a Métis charged with illegal trading in furs. Sayer is released and his confiscated furs returned, an action that

1849
Lord Elgin, Governor of the Canadas, signs the Rebellion Losses Bill, signalling the functioning of responsible government in the colony.

LOUIS RIEL AND THE MÉTIS

results in the end of the HBC's trade monopoly.

1850
A daughter, Marie, is born to Jean-Louis and Julie Riel.

1851
Louis Riel begins attending school at the convent school of the Grey Nuns in St. Boniface.

During the 1850s, Louis's father is leader of the French community in Red River. Jean-Louis Riel advocates Métis representation on the Council of Assiniboia and the use of French as well as English in the courts of Assiniboia.

1852
The Red River floods, and the waters engulf the Riel family home.

A daughter, Octavie, is born to Jean-Louis and Julie Riel.

1853
A daughter, Eulalie, is born to Jean-Louis and Julie Riel.

1854
Jean-Louis Riel sets up a gristmill on the Seine River and builds a bigger house for his family.

CANADA AND THE WORLD

William Lyon Mackenzie is pardoned and returns from the U.S.

1850
A land grant act spurs the development of railroads in the U.S.

1851
In the U.S., the *New York Times* begins publication.

Herman Melville's *Moby Dick* is published.

In Great Britain, Reuters news service is established.

London holds the first world exhibition at the new Crystal Palace.

1852
Susanna Moodie's *Roughing It in the Bush*, which describes her experience of immigration to Canada, is published in London.

Harriet Beecher Stowe's *Uncle Tom's Cabin* is a bestseller in North America and Europe.

1853
Italian composer Giuseppe Verdi writes the operas *La traviata* and *Il trovatore*.

1854
A Reciprocity Treaty inaugurates free trade between the British North American colonies and the U.S.

LOUIS RIEL AND THE MÉTIS	CANADA AND THE WORLD
A son, Charles, is born to Jean-Louis and Julie Riel.	Britain, France, and Turkey declare war on Russia in the Crimea.
Bishop Alexandre-Antonin Taché supervises the building of a combined house and school for the Christian Brothers in St. Boniface. Louis Riel attends the school.	Alfred Lord Tennyson publishes the poem, "The Charge of the Light Brigade." Florence Nightingale pioneers modern nursing.
1855 The voyageur Jean-Baptiste Lagimodière, maternal grandfather of Louis Riel, dies.	**1855** The Treaty of Paris ends the Crimean War. A world exhibition is held in Paris, France.
1857 A son, Joseph, is born to Jean-Louis and Julie Riel.	**1857** Ottawa is chosen as the capital of the Province of Canada. The British expedition led by John Palliser begins its work in western North America to determine the suitability of the HBC lands for agricultural settlement. A revolt by Indian soldiers against the British is put down but leads to the end of the British East India Company's rule of India.
1858 Louis Riel attracts the attention of Bishop Taché, who arranges for him to study for the priesthood. With two other Métis boys, he travels to Montreal. En route, he sees his father for the last time.	**1858** The Fraser River Gold Rush attracts large numbers of men, many of them Chinese. The mainland colony of British Columbia is established.

LOUIS RIEL AND THE MÉTIS

Louis attends the Collège de Montréal while the other boys go to different schools. The boys spend part of their summer vacation with the Masson family.

1859
Louis does well in his studies. The curriculum includes Latin, Greek, French, English, mathematics, philosophy, and theology.

The first steamship reaches St. Boniface.

1860
The St. Boniface Cathedral is destroyed by fire.

1861
The other Métis boys return to Red River; only Louis remains at school in Montreal.

Louis continues to spend part of his summer vacation with the Masson family each year; he becomes friends with Rodrigue Masson, a young lawyer. He spends the rest of his summer vacation time with his aunt and uncle in Mile End, on the outskirts of Montreal.

In St. Boniface, Sara Riel enters the convent of the Grey Nuns as a novice.

A daughter, Henriette, is born to Jean-Louis and Julie Riel.

CANADA AND THE WORLD

The Irish Republican (Fenian) Brotherhood is established in North America.

India becomes a crown colony of Great Britain.

1859
Charles Darwin publishes *On the Origin of Species by Means of Natural Selection*.

The *Nor'Wester* weekly newspaper is established in Red River.

1861
Abraham Lincoln is elected president of the U.S.

The American Civil War begins.

Future Canadian poet Emily Pauline Johnson is born at Chiefswood, near Brantford, Ontario.

The kingdom of Italy is formed and Victor Emmanuel II becomes King.

Louis Riel

LOUIS RIEL AND THE MÉTIS **CANADA AND THE WORLD**

1863
A son, Alexandre, is born to Jean-Louis and Julie Riel.

1864
In February, Louis Riel receives news of the death of his father.

In the summer, Louis falls in love with Marie-Julie Guernon, who lives next door to his aunt and uncle in Mile End. He begins to write love poems.

1864
In September, at the Charlotte-town Conference, delegates from five provinces of British North America discuss union under one government.

In October, they hold a second meeting, the Quebec Conference.

Louis Pasteur of France invents pasteurization.

1865
Louis Riel decides to enter a profession. He neglects his school-work and rebels against college discipline. He is expelled and goes to live with his aunt and uncle in Mile End.

He studies law in Montreal with well-known lawyer and Parti rouge supporter Rodolphe Laflamme.

1865
In the U.S., President Abraham Lincoln is assassinated; the Civil War ends.

The 13th Amendment to the U.S. Constitution abolishes slavery. The Ku Klux Klan is founded.

1866
Louis Riel and Marie-Julie Guernon sign a wedding contract and announce their forthcoming marriage. Marie-Julie's parents are outraged; within a week she breaks their engagement.

Riel leaves Montreal.

1866
The colonies of British Columbia and Vancouver Island unite.

Fenians invade Canada and are repelled by the Canadian militia and British troops at the Battle of Ridgeway.

In Europe, Prussia defeats Austria in a seven-week war.

LOUIS RIEL AND THE MÉTIS

CANADA AND THE WORLD

Swedish chemist and industrialist Alfred Nobel invents dynamite.

1867

A grasshopper plague causes distress in the Red River Settlement during 1867-1868.

The buffalo are disappearing due to overhunting; the fur trade is in decline due to a change in fashion in Europe. Many Métis in Red River have turned to full-time farming.

1867

The British North America Act establishes the Dominion of Canada, uniting Nova Scotia, New Brunswick, Quebec, and Ontario; John A. Macdonald is elected prime minister and is knighted by Queen Victoria.

The Clear Grits and the Rouges unite to become the Liberal Party of Canada.

The U.S. buys Alaska from Russia for $7.2 million.

1868

Louis Riel returns from working in the U.S. to live in the Red River Settlement. His mother and family have moved to the parish of St. Vital on the east bank of the Red River, near the Lagimodière family. Riel works on the farm and tries to help his family.

Charles Mair arrives in Red River as paymaster for the work crew on the Dawson Road to be built between Upper Fort Garry and Lake of the Woods.

1868

The HBC relinquishes its trading monopoly and transfers title of Rupert's Land to Canada in exchange for £300,000 ($1.5 million), the lands around its trading posts, and 1/20th of the good agricultural lands on the Prairies.

Completion of a railway linking St. Paul and eastern North America facilitates access to the Red River Settlement.

1869

In January, a letter of Charles Mair's giving an account of Red River is published in the Toronto *Globe*. He hopes to encourage immigration from Ontario.

1869

The Dominion of Canada is scheduled to take control of Rupert's Land on December 1. Prime Minister Sir John A. Macdonald sends William McDougall as first Canadian

LOUIS RIEL AND THE MÉTIS

In February, Louis Riel writes a letter to the editor of a Montreal newspaper, *Le Nouveau Monde.* He asserts that Mair has not told the truth about Red River and its people.

In June, Charles Mair and John Snow, an Ontarian in charge of building the Dawson Road, begin pacing out lots on Métis land but are driven off.

In July, the Métis hold a meeting and choose two captains to arrange patrols and keep strangers off Métis land.

In August, Canadian surveyors led by Colonel Dennis arrive in the Red River Settlement.

Louis Riel addresses a crowd from the steps of the rebuilt St. Boniface Cathedral. He warns them the Canadian government has sent no guarantees the land rights of the inhabitants of Red River will be respected after takeover.

On October 1, Riel meets with Colonel Dennis of the survey party. Dennis assures him the Canadian government plans to grant free titles to all existing landholders. Riel is not convinced.

On October 6, he writes a letter to a newspaper, *Le Courrier de Saint-Hyacinthe*, in hope of sparking

CANADA AND THE WORLD

lieutenant-governor of the North-West Territories.

The Suez Canal opens, allowing transportation between Europe and Asia without circumnavigation of Africa.

The first transcontinental railroad in the U.S. is completed when the Central Pacific and Union Pacific lines meet.

LOUIS RIEL AND THE MÉTIS

CANADA AND THE WORLD

sympathy in Quebec for the Métis cause.

On October 11, the survey party begins to survey the property of Édouard Marion, a Métis farmer. Riel and others stand on the survey chain and demand that they stop. The surveyors withdraw.

On October 16, at a meeting at St. Norbert, the Métis elect representatives to a new organization called the National Committee. John Bruce is elected president and Louis Riel secretary.

On October 17, the Committee builds a roadblock. On October 21, they send a letter to order Lieutenant-Governor McDougall not to enter the territory without permission of the National Committee of the Métis.

On November 2, Métis men under orders from the National Committee confront William McDougall just north of the border. They escort him back to the U.S. the next morning.

Meanwhile, Riel and 120 men take control of Upper Fort Garry.

Riel and the Métis draw up a List of Rights.

On December 8, Riel issues the Declaration of the People of Rupert's Land and the North-West,

LOUIS RIEL AND THE MÉTIS	CANADA AND THE WORLD

which establishes a provisional government. John Bruce is declared president. Riel replaces him later in December.

Members of the Canadian party, led by John Schulz, are disarmed by the Métis and imprisoned in Fort Garry.

1870

On January 9, a small group of Riel's prisoners, including Charles Mair and Thomas Scott, escape from jail.

Scott, an Irish Orangeman who is contemptuous of the Métis, is recaptured on February 17.

On March 3, Thomas Scott is tried before a Métis council, convicted, and sentenced to death. He is executed the next day by firing squad.

On March 6, the joint provisional government meets for the first time.

On March 23 and 24, delegates leave for Ottawa to negotiate with the government of Canada.

On April 9, Riel proclaims the end of martial law.

On June 25, the provisional government (renamed the legislative assembly) accepts the Manitoba Act unanimously. Manitoba becomes a province on July 15.

1870

In May, the Manitoba Act creates Canada's fifth province; it recognizes French and English as official languages and allows funding of Protestant and Catholic schools by public taxation.

Section 31 of the Manitoba Act promises to distribute 1.4 million acres (3,459,000 hectares) of land among Métis children.

Section 32 promises the Métis will receive title to the lands they already occupy.

Prime Minister Macdonald sends soldiers under Colonel Wolseley to Red River on a "mission of peace."

The province of Ontario offers a $5000 reward for the capture of those responsible for the death of Thomas Scott.

France declares war on Prussia.

In India, the Calcutta to Bombay railway link makes travel across the subcontinent possible.

LOUIS RIEL AND THE MÉTIS

In August, Colonel Wolseley and his troops reach Red River; the troops are dominated by young Ontario Orangemen. Riel flees across the U.S. border. He spends the fall and winter in St. Joseph, near the border.

1871
In February, Riel is seriously ill with fever and swollen joints.

In May, he returns to St. Vital.

Sara Riel travels to Île-à-la-Crosse as a missionary nun.

Riel makes a speech in honour of Bishop Taché, who has been made an archbishop.

In October, without disclosing his identity, Riel meets Lieutenant-Governor Archibald in St. Boniface.

In December, masked men break into the Riel homestead and ransack it while Louis is away at a meeting.

Between 1871 and 1884, as many as 4000 Métis people migrate west to the Saskatchewan territory.

1872
In February, Riel and Ambroise Lépine agree to Prime Minister Macdonald's request that they leave the country. They travel to St. Paul in the U.S.

CANADA AND THE WORLD

1871
British Columbia joins Confederation as the sixth Canadian province on the promise that a transcontinental railway will be built within ten years.

Sandford Fleming accepts the position of Chief Engineer of the proposed Pacific Railway.

Treaty No. 1 and Treaty No. 2 are signed between the government of Canada and Saulteaux (Plains Ojibwa) and Cree First Nations.

Emily Carr, future painter and writer, is born in Victoria, B.C.

The Franco-Prussian War ends with Prussia victorious. William I, King of Prussia, is proclaimed German Emperor; Germany is finally a unified nation.

1872
Quebec Liberal Honoré Mercier and others found the Parti national; Mercier is elected to the House of Commons.

LOUIS RIEL AND THE MÉTIS

Lépine returns to Red River. Riel writes about the Scott affair for a Quebec newspaper. He then returns to Red River and begins to campaign for the nomination in the Provencher riding.

In September, Louis Riel refuses the nomination in Provencher riding. George-Etienne Cartier is elected by acclamation. Riel expects Cartier to help resolve the Métis land claims issue and to speed an amnesty for himself and Ambroise Lépine.

1873

In January, Louis is shaken by the death of his sister, Marie. He goes into a religious retreat in March and April.

In May, Riel learns that George-Étienne Cartier has died. He decides to run in the byelection in Provencher riding.

In September, a warrant is issued in Winnipeg for the arrest of Louis Riel and his second-in-command, Ambroise Lépine.

In October, Louis Riel is elected as a Member of Parliament by acclamation in the federal byelection.

He goes to Montreal, where old friends introduce him to influential people. He does not enter

CANADA AND THE WORLD

Canada passes the Dominion Lands Act to administer and manage the public lands of Manitoba and the North-West Territories and to encourage settlement.

The *Manitoba Free Press* is founded.

In France, Jules Verne publishes *Le tour du monde en quatre-vingts jours*, which is translated and published in English the following year as *Around the World in Eighty Days*.

1873

Prince Edward Island joins Confederation.

Treaty No. 3 is signed between the government of Canada and the Saulteaux (Plains Ojibwa).

In the Cypress Hills, after a quarrel with an Assiniboine band over horses, American whisky traders cross the border and raid the Assiniboine village. Thirty-six Assiniboine people are killed, and the village is burned.

Canada establishes the North West Mounted Police (NWMP) to keep the peace.

Winnipeg, Manitoba is incorporated as a city.

LOUIS RIEL AND THE MÉTIS

Parliament in Ottawa for fear of arrest.

In December, Riel stays with the Barnabé family in Keeseville, New York.

1874
In January, Riel is in Montreal.

In February, Riel retains his seat in the general election; in March he goes to Ottawa, signs the register, but is expelled from Parliament.

He returns to Keeseville.

He travels to St. Paul and Quebec. He speaks at protest meetings and visits influential people who might help him obtain amnesty.

In September, Riel is again elected to Parliament by the voters of Provencher.

In November, Ambroise Lépine is convicted of murder and sentenced to hang.

In December, on a mountaintop in Washington, D.C., Riel has a vision and receives a heavenly message concerning his mission as the leader of his people.

CANADA AND THE WORLD

None of the 1.4 million acres promised under the Manitoba Act has been allotted to the Métis.

In Ottawa, Prime Minister Sir John A. Macdonald resigns over charges of bribery; the new Liberal prime minister, Alexander Mackenzie, calls a general election.

1874
Pressure cooking, a new procedure for sterilizing canned foods, is introduced in the U.S. by Isaac Solomon.

Treaty No. 4 is signed between the government of Canada and the Cree, Saulteaux (Plains Ojibwa), and Assiniboine peoples.

Section 32 of the Manitoba Act is amended to require proof of significant improvements to the land occupied before ownership will be granted.

To satisfy land claims under the Manitoba Act, the Canadian government issues certificates called "scrip," which can be exchanged for Crown land in any area open for settlement.

Scrip is issued to Métis children and heads of households and to "original white settlers" who came to Red River during the Selkirk Settlement years.

LOUIS RIEL AND THE MÉTIS

1875

In January, the Governor General of Canada commutes Lépine's sentence to two years' imprisonment.

In February, amnesty is granted for all participants in the Red River Resistance. However, Riel and Lépine are to be banished for five years and have their political rights suspended for life. Riel is again expelled from Parliament.

In December, Riel is in Washington, D.C., where he speaks with President Ulysses S. Grant.

Riel has a powerful religious experience while attending mass. Later, he sees a vision of the Virgin Mary and believes the Holy Spirit has spoken to him. He declares that he is a prophet. His mood swings and strange behaviour are interpreted as insanity.

Marie-Anne (Gaboury) Lagimodière, maternal grandmother of Louis Riel, dies at the age of 95.

1876

Riel's uncle, John Lee, smuggles him across the border to Montreal.

In March, under the name Louis R. David, he is admitted to an asylum for the insane, the Hospice de St. Jean-de-Dieu, at Longue Pointe.

CANADA AND THE WORLD

1875

The government of Canada grants amnesty to Riel but banishes him for five years from "Her Majesty's Dominions."

In the U.S., Mary Baker Eddy writes *Science and Health*, which will lead to the founding of the Christian Science movement.

The Theosophical Society is founded in New York by Madame H.P. Blavatsky and others.

Treaty No. 5 between the government of Canada and the Cree and Saulteaux (Plains Ojibwa) is signed.

The first organized game of indoor ice hockey is played in Canada at Montreal's Victoria Skating Rink.

1876

Dr. Emily Stowe founds the Toronto Women's Literary Club, Canada's first suffrage group.

Treaty No. 6 is signed between the government of Canada and the Plains and Wood Cree.

LOUIS RIEL AND THE MÉTIS

In May, he is sent to the Beauport asylum near Quebec City. He spends his time writing of his mission and creates a new faith, the Catholic, Apostolic, and Vital Church of the Shining Mountains. He writes that the Métis are God's chosen people, and God has chosen him to be the prophet of the New World.

In November, Archbishop Taché visits Riel in the asylum.

1877
Riel writes letters to his family from the asylum.

1878
In January, Riel is released from the asylum. He visits the Barnabé family in Keeseville. In the spring, he rents farmland and plants crops. He and Evelina Barnabé fall in love.

CANADA AND THE WORLD

The first Indian Act is passed by Canada's Parliament. Indian agents take control of reserves. Education is the responsibility of the Department of Indian Affairs.

Lt. Col. George Custer and the soldiers of the American 7th Cavalry lose the Battle of the Little Big Horn and are massacred by the Sioux and Cheyenne.

Alexander Graham Bell registers the first patent for the telephone.

In Germany, Nikolaus Otto invents the internal combustion engine.

1877
Sioux Chief Crazy Horse surrenders, marking the end of the American Plains Indian Wars. Sioux Chief Sitting Bull leads his Dakota band north to Canada to escape the U.S. army.

The Blackfoot Nation, led by Chief Crowfoot, signs Treaty No. 7 with the government of Canada.

British Queen Victoria is proclaimed Empress of India.

1878
In England, William Booth establishes the Salvation Army to take the Christian message to poor, homeless, and destitute people.

LOUIS RIEL AND THE MÉTIS	**CANADA AND THE WORLD**

After a poor harvest, Riel goes to New York City to look for work, then to St. Paul, Minnesota. He writes poems and love letters to Evelina Barnabé.

Charles Taze Russell in the U.S. founds the Jehovah's Witnesses movement.

Pope Pius IX dies at Rome and is succeeded by Pope Leo XIII.

1879

In January, Riel is in St. Joseph, where his mother, brothers, and sisters visit him.

Riel stops writing to Evelina Barnabé.

In August, he travels to the Saskatchewan territory to meet with Chief Sitting Bull at Wood Mountain.

Riel spends the winter in a Métis hunting camp, near Milk River, Montana. He is elected *chef du camp*.

1879

In the U.S., Thomas A. Edison invents the electric light bulb.

First Nations people are starving on the reserves on Canada's Prairies due to the disappearance of the buffalo and crop failures.

1880

In the spring, Riel moves farther south with a group of 30-40 buffalo hunters.

He gets permission from the army commander at Fort Benton for his group to spend the winter on a nearby reservation. The winter is harsh.

Riel is the spokesperson for the Métis of Montana between 1880 and 1884.

1880

A contract for the construction of a railway from Montreal to the Pacific is awarded to the Canadian Pacific Railway (CPR) syndicate.

In both Canada and the U.S., the buffalo have been hunted almost to extinction.

The second Indian Act is passed by Canada's Parliament.

LOUIS RIEL AND THE MÉTIS

1881
On April 27, Louis Riel marries Marguerite Monet *dit* Bellehumeur. Their "country" marriage will be sanctioned by a priest the following year.

In the autumn, Louis and Marguerite move with the Métis to Rocky Point on the Missouri River. He sets up a small business as a travelling trader.

1882
In May, a son, Jean, is born to Louis and Marguerite Riel.

Grasshoppers again destroy crops and cause hardship in the Red River area.

1883
In March, Riel becomes an American citizen.

In April, he takes the job of schoolteacher at St. Peter's Mission in Montana, to begin in September.

In June, he travels to Manitoba to see his family at St. Vital and to investigate the situation with land claims and scrip.

In July, Riel attends the wedding of his sister Henriette to Jean-Marie Poitras. He sees family members and many old friends. He returns to Montana in August.

CANADA AND THE WORLD

1881
In Russia, Czar Alexander II is assassinated.

Large numbers of Chinese labourers are brought to Canada to build the CPR through the Rocky Mountains.

1882
Macdonald's Conservative party is returned to power in Canada's federal election.

The U.S. bans Chinese immigration for ten years.

1883
Honoré Mercier becomes leader of the provincial Liberal party in Quebec.

There is again widespread starvation amongst the First Nations on the reserves of Canada's Prairies.

In the U.S, Buffalo Bill Cody organizes his "Wild West Show," which will tour Europe and the U.S. until 1916.

The Paris to Istanbul Orient Express railway completes its first run.

The spectacular eruption of Krakatoa Volcano on Pulau Island

LOUIS RIEL AND THE MÉTIS	CANADA AND THE WORLD

In September, the Riels' second child, a daughter named Marie-Angélique, is born.

(now part of Indonesia) sends volcanic dust around the world.

Riel begins his teaching job in November.

In December, his sister Sara dies of tuberculosis.

1884

In June, Gabriel Dumont and a delegation of Métis arrive to meet with Louis Riel. They have come 1100 kilometres from the Saskatchewan territory to ask him to help the Métis obtain their legal rights from the Canadian government.

Louis Riel and his family travel to Batoche in the South Saskatchewan River Valley with the Métis delegation.

In December, a petition drafted by Louis Riel and his supporters is sent to the Governor General with copies to the dominion government.

1884

International Standard Time is adopted at the International Prime Meridian Conference convened by Sandford Fleming in Washington, D.C.

Chief Big Bear attempts to unite the Northern Cree; the government of Canada refuses to negotiate with him and he loses the support of his followers.

The dominion government bans the potlatch on Canada's West Coast; the ban will last for sixty years.

1885

In January the dominion government sets up a Land Claims Commission to create a list of Saskatchewan Métis people who might receive land grants.

On March 2, Riel asks Father André for the support of the Church for a provisional government to renegoti-

1885

On March 23, Prime Minister Macdonald orders General Middleton to lead an armed force from Canada to the Prairies. The newly built Canadian Pacific Railway (CPR) transports soldiers to Fort Qu'Appelle.

LOUIS RIEL AND THE MÉTIS

ate the rights of the Métis people and is refused.

On March 7, the Métis of St. Laurent learn the Canadian government has refused most of them title to the land they have claimed.

On March 19, Riel declares a provisional government to be called the Exovedate.

On March 26, at Duck Lake, the Métis, led by Gabriel Dumont, clash with the NWMP led by Superintendant Crozier.

On March 30, Cree warriors from Poundmaker's band attack the town of Battleford. Residents take refuge in Fort Battleford.

On April 2, Cree warriors from Big Bear's band kill nine whites at Frog Lake. On April 14, they besiege and then burn down Fort Pitt.

On April 24, at Fish Creek, the Métis under Dumont fight the Canadian forces to a standstill.

On May 9, the Battle of Batoche begins.

On May 12, Canadian troops storm the village, and the battle ends with the defeat of the Métis.

On May 15, Riel surrenders to General Middleton. Gabriel

CANADA AND THE WORLD

The raids by First Nations warriors, in which settlers and priests in Saskatchewan are killed, arouse hatred of Riel in English Canada.

Chinese people are denied the right to vote in Canadian federal elections; upon entering the country, new Chinese immigrants must pay a fifty-dollar head tax under the Chinese Immigration Act.

The CPR is completed; in November, the Last Spike is driven at Craigallachie in British Columbia.

LOUIS RIEL AND THE MÉTIS

Dumont rides for the Montana border.

On May 23, Riel is imprisoned in a small cell in the Regina NWMP headquarters.

On July 6, he is formally charged with high treason; his trial begins on July 20.

On August 1, Riel is found guilty and sentenced to death. His lawyers appeal his sentence.

On October 21, Marguerite Riel gives birth to a boy, who dies after two hours. Riel mourns the loss of his son.

Public pressure from Quebec delays the execution, but on November 16, in Regina, Louis Riel is hanged.

CANADA AND THE WORLD

1992
The House of Commons declares Louis Riel to be one of the founders of Manitoba.

Sources Consulted

ASSOCIATION OF MÉTIS AND NON-STATUS INDIANS OF SASKATCHEWAN. *Louis Riel: Justice Must Be Done.* Winnipeg: Manitoba Métis Federation Press, 1979.

BARKWELL, Lawrence J., Leah DORION, and Darron R. PRÉFONTAINE (eds.) *Métis Legacy: a Métis Historiography and Annotated Bibliography.* Winnipeg: Pemmican Publications, 2001.

BARROW, F. Laurie and James B. WALDRON (eds.) *1885 and After. Native Society in Transition.* Regina: University of Regina Press, 1986.

BOULTON, Major Charles A. *I Fought Riel. A Military Memoir.* Toronto: Lorimer, 1985.

BRAZ, Albert. *The False Traitor: Louis Riel in Canadian Culture.* Toronto: University of Toronto Press, 2003.

BROWN, Chester. *Louis Riel: a Comic-strip Biography.* Montreal: Drawn and Quarterly Publications, 2003.

BUMSTED, J.M. *Louis Riel v. Canada.* Winnipeg: Great Plains Publications, 2001.

———. *The Red River Rebellion.* Winnipeg: Watson & Dwyer Publishing Ltd., 1996.

CHARLEBOIS, Peter. *The Life of Louis Riel*. Toronto: NC Press, 1978.

CREIGHTON, Donald. *John A. Macdonald. The Young Politician. The Old Chieftain*. Toronto: University of Toronto press, 1998.

FLANAGAN, Thomas. *Louis 'David' Riel: Prophet of the New World*. Toronto: University of Toronto Press, 1979.

————. *Riel and the Rebellion 1885 Reconsidered*. Saskatoon: Western Producer Prairie Books, 1983.

FRIESEN, John W. *The Riel/real Story*. Ottawa: Borealis Press, 1996.

HOWARD, Joseph Kinsey. *Strange Empire: Louis Riel and the Métis People*. Toronto: James, Laws and Samuel, 1952.

JORDAN, Mary. *To Louis from Your Sister Who Loves You, Sara Riel*. Toronto: Griffin House, 1974.

LUSSIER, Antoine S. *Riel and the Métis. Riel Mini-Conference Papers*. Winnipeg: Manitoba Métis Federation Press, 1979.

MARTEL, Gilles. *Le messianisme de Louis Riel.* Waterloo: Wilfrid Laurier University Press, 1984.

NEERING, Rosemary. *Louis Riel*. Don Mills: Fitzhenry & Whiteside, 1977.

PANNEKOEK, Frits. *A Snug Little Flock. The Social Origins of the Riel Resistance of 1869-70*. Winnipeg: Watson & Dwyer Publishing Ltd., 1991.

RIEL, Louis. *The Collected Writings of Louis Riel*. Volumes I-V. Edmonton: University of Alberta Press, 1985.

SIGGINS, Maggie. *Riel. A Life of Revolution*. Toronto: HarperCollins Publishers Ltd., 1994.

SPRAGUE, D.N. *Canada and the Métis, 1969-1885.* Waterloo: Wilfrid Laurier University Press, 1988.

STANLEY, George F.G. *Louis Riel.* Toronto: McGraw-Hill Ryerson Limited, 1963.

TRÉMAUDAN, Auguste Henri de. *Histoire de la nation Métisse dans l'Ouest canadien.* Saint Boniface: Editions du Blé, 1979.

WOODSTOCK, George. *Gabriel Dumont.* Edmonton: Hurtig Publishing, 1975.

Index

Numbers in *italics* indicate pages of photographs or illustrations.

Americans, 10, 60, 82, 92, 112, 143
American border, 48, 78, 135, 166, 173, 175, 176, 178, 184
American government, 143, 179
amnesty (promised to Riel), 68-71, 73, 79, 80, 82, 84-88, 90, 108, 126, 127, 155, 176, 177, 178
André, Father Alexis, 123, 125-127, 139, 142, 145, 149-152, 182
Archibald, Lieutenant-Governor A.G., 72, 73, 81, 82, 155, 175
Assiniboia, 161, 162
Assiniboine River, 51
Au Sable River, 105

Bannatyne, Annie, 35
Bannatyne, A.G., 61, 63
Barnabé, Evelina, 89, 103, 105, 106, 108, 109, 113, 114, 146, 179, 180
Barnabé, Fabien, 87, 96, 103, 106, 108
Barnabé family, 96, 105, 106, 177, 179
Batoche, 115, 127-129, 133-135, 182
Battle of Batoche, 134, 135, 183
Battleford, 131, 183
Beauport Asylum, 98, 101-103, 140, 179
Big Bear, 131, 182, 183
Black, John, 62
Botkin, Alexander, 112
Boulton, Major Charles, 66
Bourget, Bishop Ignace, 89, 92, 98, 100, 143

Breland, Pascal, 34
Britain and British, 71, 78, 79, 159, 163, 166. *See also* Great Britain; England.
Bruce, John, 43, 47-49, 58, 173, 174
buffalo, 3, 8, 19, 31, 34, 110, 133, 165, 171, 180
Bunn, Thomas, 59

Canada, 1-4, *28*, 30, 33, 34, 42, 43, 46, 49, 53-56, 59, 61, 62, 66-68, 70-72, 78, 81, 91, 92, *104*, 117, 122, 125-128, 130, 135, 141, 155-157, 162, 163, 165-168, 170, 171, 174, 178, 179, 183
Canadian Confederation, 69, 88, 175, 176
Canadian government, 42, 44, 45, 47, 50, 53, 55, 57, 59, 62, 70, 79-81, 85-87, 124, 141-143, 146, 148, 155, 156, 172, 174, 175, 176, 179, 182, 183
Canadian Illustrated News, 76
Canadian Pacific Railway (CPR), 131, 132, 180, 181, 182, 183
Canadian Parliament, 56, 57, 69, 84, 86-88, 90, 99, 106, 107, 126, 177, 179, 180
Canadian party, 33, 35, 56, 58, 174
Canadian troops, 131-134, 136, 155, 182, 183
Canadian West, 8, 27, 34, 47, 66, 108, 109, 127, 156, 161
Canadians, 1, 45, 56-58, 60, 66, 72, 79, 82
Carlton Trail, 130
Carrière, Damase, 115

Cartier, George-Étienne, 21, 25, 26, 71, 84, 176; death, 85, 126, 176
Catholic, Apostolic, and Vital Church of the Shining Mountains, 100, 102, 113, 117, 156, 179
Catholic Church, 8, 21, 26, 100, 142, 143, 182
Chapleau, J.A., 148
Chapleau, Sheriff, 150
Chicago, 17, 143
Chipewyan People, 8, 162
Christian Brothers, 12, 168
Clarke, Lawrence, 128
Cleveland, Grover, 143
Collège de Montréal, 18, 24, 25, 148, 169
Conservative Party of Canada, 71, 147, 181
Convention of Forty, 61
Council of Assiniboia, 9, 34, 49, 55, 56, 167
Le Courrier de Saint-Hyacinthe, 46, 172
Cowan, William, 51
Cree language, 9, 12, 58, 113
Cree People, 130, 131, 175, 177, 178, 182, 183
Crozier, Superintendant Leif, 129, 130, 183

Dawson Road, 171, 172
Declaration of the People of Rupert's Land and the North-West, 58, 173, 174
Dease, William, 43
Democratic Party (U.S.), 112
Dennis, Colonel John S., 44-46, 57, 58, 172
Desjardins, Alphonse, 86, 142
Dewdney, Lieutenant-Governor, 147, 148

drought, 35, 41, 72
Dubuc, Joseph, 72, 80, 81, 85, 88, 99, 107, 115
Duck Lake, 129, 130, 183
Dumont, Édouard, 133
Dumont, Gabriel, 71, *104*, 116, 129-135, 155, 182, 183, 184; birth, 164
Dumont, Isidore, 130

England, 108, 146, 163. *See also* Great Britain; Britain and British
English-speaking settlers, 3-4, 9, 33, 34, 43, 44, 53, 54, 55, 56, 60, 62, 72, 73, 91, 115, 122, 125, 129, 131, 171, 183
executioner, 151, 152
Exovedate. *See* provisional government of 1885

Fenians, 70, 81, 106, 125, 169, 170
First Nations peoples, 2, 12, 34, 43, 58, 109, 123, 124, 131, 164, 175, 176, 177, 178, 179, 180, 181, 183
Fiset, Jean-Baptiste-Romuald, 86-88, 142
Fish Creek, 121, 133, 134, 183
Fort Battleford, 183
Fort Benton, 110, 180
Fort Carlton, 128-130
Fort Garry, 9, 29, 47, 51, 52, 53, 54, 58, 63, 65-69, 73, 76, 78, 116, 171, 173, 174
Fort Qu'Appelle, 132, 182
Fourmond, Father, 125, 128, 139, 142
French Canada, 12, 19
French-Canadian nationalism, 21, 156
French Canadians, 2, 8, 9, 22, 30, 86, 87, 90-92, 142, 150

French language, 12, 26, 58, 67, 167, 174
Frog Lake, 131, 183
fur trade, 10, 11, 25, 34, 52, 69, 161, 162, 167, 168, 171

Gibson, Sheriff, 150
Globe (Toronto), 35, 171
Goulet, 34
Governor General, 71, 90, 178, 182
Grandin, Father Vidal, 124
Grant, Cuthbert, 163
Grant, Ulysses S., 92, 178
grasshopper plagues, 31, 35, 41, 69, 72, 171, 181
Great Britain, 162, 164, 165, 169. *See also* Britain and British; England
Grey Nuns, 12, 17, 20, 24, 29, 32, 80, 167, 169
Guernon, Marie-Julie, *16*, 21, 24-26, 106, 170
Guernon family, 24, 26, 106, 169

Hospice de St. Jean-de-Dieu, 97, 178
House of Commons, 87, 88, 90, 156, 175, 184
Howard, Dr. Henry, 97, 98
Hudson's Bay Company (HBC), 2, 8-10, 22, 33, 34, 42, 43, 46, 47, 52, 53, 54, 58, 61, 66, 69, 128, 130, 159, 160-163, 167, 168, 171
Hull, 86

Île-à-la-Crosse, 85, 107, 163, 165, 175
Indianapolis, 91
Ireland, Bishop John, 106
Irish, 19, 65, 70, 92, 161, 162, 166
Irvine, Colonel A.G., 149

Jukes, Dr. Augustus, 147

Keeseville, 87, 89, *94*, 103, 106, 177, 179
Kildonan, 65, 66

Lachapelle, Ernest, 86, 97, 102
Lac La Biche, 131
Laflamme, Rodolphe, 26, 170
Lagimodière family, 9, 10, 12, 31, 160, 161, 165, 168, 171
Lake Winnipeg, 8
Land Claims Commission, 126, 182, 183
land rights (Métis), 2-4, 42-49, 55-57, 60, 69, 72, 81, 107, 109, 115, 117, 122-124, 126-128, 156, 163, 172-174, 176, 177, 181, 182, 183. *See also*, Scrip
Lavallée, Louis (brother-in-law), 106
Lavell, Dr. M., 147, 148
Lee, John (uncle), 24, 96, 97, 101, 169, 170, 178
Lee, Lucie, *née* Riel (aunt), 21, 24, 169, 170
LeFloch, Father, 78
legislative assembly, 72, 82, 85, 174
Lépine, Ambroise, 53, 77, 78, 83, 85, 86, 88-90, 99, 107, 108, 175, 176, 177, 178
Lépine, Maxime, 107
List of Rights (Métis), 56, 61, 62, 68, 70, *154*, 173
London, England, 10, 142, 167
Longue Pointe, *94*, 97, 98, 178
Louis Riel Day, 156, 157
Lower Canada, 160, 163, 164, 165

Macdonald, Prime Minister John A., 59, 71, 83, 126, 131, 147, 148, 162, 171, 174, 175, 177, 181, 182
MacDowell, Andrew, 125, 126

Mactavish, William, 46, 47, 49, 50, 54, 55, 61
Mair, Charles, 35, 36, 42, 45, 65, 70, 171, 172, 174
Mallet, Edmund, 90, 95
Manitoba, 69, 72, 78, 80, 81, 89, 91, 92, 114, 115, 122, 125, 139, 141, 142, 153, 156, 174, 176, 181, 184
Le Manitoba, 122
Manitoba Act, 69, 72, 78, 81, 82, 125-127, 173, 177
Manitoba government, 82, 125, *154*
Marion, Édouard, 1, 173
Marion family and farm, 2, 3, 46, 106
Massinahican, 113
Masson, Marie-Geneviève-Sophie, 20, 21, 24
Masson, Rodrigue, 21, 86, 88, 142, 169
Masson family, 21, 169
McDougall, Daniel, 15, 18, 20, 168, 169
McDougall, William, 44, 47-49, 53-57, 62, 68, 171, 173
McWilliams, Father, 151, 152
Mercier, Honoré, 156, 175, 181
Métis People, *xiv*, 1-4, 7-9, 12, 24, *28*, 30, 34, 35, 42-46, 49, 55, 56, 66-70, 72, 79, 8-82, 84, 86, 91, 92, 95, 99-101, 107, 109-112, 114, 116, 117, 121-128, 130-135, 139-142, 153, 155, 162-165, 171-175, 177-183
and alcohol, 109, 110, 112
armed force, 47, 48, 51, 53, 54, 56-58 61, 62, 65, 76, 82, 104, 129, 130, 131, 133, 134, 174
flag, 58, 69
government, 42, 45, 47, 55, 58, 60, 61, *64*, 65, 66, 68, 69, 72, 93,
173, 174, 183. *See also* provisional government
opposition to HBC, 10, 11, 43, 54, 163, 166, 167
See also: land rights; North-West Rebellion; Red River Resistance
Middleton, General Frederick, *120*, 131-136, 182, 183
military expedition against Métis (1870), 55, 70, 72-74, 77, 79, 125, 174, 175
Mile End, 21, 23, 24, 26, 169, 170
Milk River, 109, 180
Minneapolis, 30
Minnesota, 106
Mississippi River, 17
Missouri River, 112, 122, 181
mixed-bloods (English-speaking), 9, 33, 34, 35, 55, 61, 62, 122, 129, 131
Montana, *104*, 109, 110, 114, 121, 127, 135, *158*, 180, 181, 184
Montreal, *6*, 13, 17, 18, 21, 25, 27, 30, 36, 72, 86-89, 96, 98, 100, 160, 162, 164, 168, 169, 170, 172, 176, 177, 178, 180
Mormon faith, 156, 166
Moulin, Father, 129
Mousseau, Joseph-Alfred, 88

National Committee, 47, 48, 173
Nault, André, 1, 2
Nault, Napoléon, 115, 126, 135
Nebraska, 103
New England, 89, 90
New York City, 106, 161, 180
New York State, 86, 94, 177
Nolin, Charles, 60-62, 121, 128, 137, 139
North Saskatchewan River, 131
North Saskatchewan region, 161, 163

North-West, 13, 48, 53, 56, 58, 69, 91, 100, *104*, 117, 139, 141, 163, 165, 173
North·West Company, 160, 162, 163
North-West Council, 125
North West Mounted Police, 128-130, 141, 147, 176, 183
North-West Rebellion, 120, 132-136, 140, *120*, 155, 164
North-West Territories (1870-1905), 91, 147, 172, 176
Le Nouveau Monde, 36, 86, 172

Oak Point, 44
O'Donoghue, William Bernard, 70, 73, 77-79, 81, 82
Ontario, 9, 33, 34, 70, 71, *76*, 82, 83, 88, 91, 141, 142, 147, 153, 156, 159, 160, 171, 174, 175
Orange Order and Orangemen, 70, 83, 98, 153, 174, 175
Ottawa, 68, 86, 168, 174, 177
Ouellette, Moïse, 135

Parti bleu, 21, 25
Parti national, 175
Parti Québécois, 156
Parti rouge, 166, 170, 171
Pembina, 48, 49, 53, 56, 57, 77, 78
Pepin, Simon, 112
Portage la Prairie, 65, 66
Primeau, Father, 95, 96
Prince Albert, 122, 123, 130
Privy Council, 146
Proclamation to the People of the North-West, 69
provisional government of 1869-1870, 58-63, *64*, 65-72, 174
provisional government of 1885 (Exovedate), 129, 132, 133, 183
Protestants and Protestantism, 9, 70, 83, 125, 153, 174

Provencher riding, 84, 85, 89, 99, 176, 177,

Qu'Appelle road, 133
Quebec, 46, 70, 83, 84, 86, 89, 139, 142, 146-148, 156, 159, 160, 166, 171, 173, 175-177, 181, 184
Quebec City, 98, 179
Quinn, 19, 20

Red Lake, 17
Red River, 11, 29, 30, 51, 163, 167, 171
Red River carts, *xiv*, 7, 8, 15, 34, 42, 69, 109, 117
Red River Resistance, 44, 46-51, *52*, 53, 57-68, 71, 88, 90, 115, 141, 172-174, 178
Red River Settlement, 2, 3, 8-10, 20, *28*, 29-33, 35, 36, 41-44, 46-49, 53-57, 59, 61, 62, 65-73, 78, 82, 84, 85, 87, 90, 93, 101, 107, 114, 151, 155, 161-165, 167, 169, 171, 172, 174-176, 181;
population of, 166
Regina, 137, *138*, 184
Republican Party (U.S.), 112
Richer, Father J.B.E., 95
Riel, Alexandre (brother), 31, 33, 77, 80, 106, 170, 180
Riel, Charles (brother), 12, 14, 31-33, 80, 106, 168, 180
Riel, Eulalie (sister), 12, 14, 80, 106, 167, 180
Riel, Henriette (sister), 31, 80, 106, 114, 146, 149, 150, 160, 180, 181
Riel, Jean (son), *104*, 112, 135, 143, 145, 147, 149, 181
Riel, Jean-Louis (father), 8-11, 13, 17, 32, 48, 50, 114, 165, 166, 167, 168, 169, 170; activist for

Métis,11, 48, 50, 166, 167; death, 22, 170; education, 163; works for HBC, 164
Riel, Joseph (brother), 12, 14, 31, 33, 80, 106, 110, 122, 144, 168, 180
Riel, Julie, *née* Lagimodière (mother), 9-13, 30-32, 80, 101, 106, 143, 144, 149, 150, 166-170, 180; birth, 164; marriage, 10, 165
Riel, Louis:
American citizenship, 110, 114, 181
appearance, 1, 12, 31, 34, 41, *158*
arrest warrant for, 85, 86, 176, 177
banishment, 90,178
birth, 10, 165
Catholic upbringing, 9-11, 18, 19, 21
childhood, *6*, 7-15, 17-20
committed to asylums, 97, 98, 101-103, 140, 178, 179
death, 152, 156, 184
education, 12, 13, 18, 19, 21, 23, 24, 43, 45, 167-170
elected Member of Parliament, 86, 87, 89, 176, 177
exile in U.S., 83, 84, 89-93, 95, 96, 103-117, 155, 175
expelled from college, 24, 170
expelled from Parliament, 88, 90, 177, 178
fiery style, 40, 48, 89, 153
hatred of bullying, 19, 20
ill health 67, 80, 175
law clerk, *16*, 26, 170
love of learning, 13
marriage, 112, 181
president of provisional government, 58, 60, 61, 66, 68, 72, 174

price on his head, 83
religious belief, 23, 23, 99, 113, 124, 125
religious visions, 95-98, 100, 116, 132-134, 142, 143, 146, 155, 156, 178, 179
schoolteacher, 115, 116, 122, 181, 182
secretary of National Committee 45, 47, 48, 55-57, 173
sense of divine mission, 4, 90, 92, 93, 95, 96, 100, 102, 116, 123, 124, 129
trial, 137, *138*, 139, 140, 141, 184
uses additional name "David," 85, 90, 97, 150, 178
writings, 21, 23, 25, 36, 37, 46, 91, 98-100, 102, 103, 105, 106, 110-113, 115, 122, 124, 141, 143-147, 149, 150, 170, 172, 176, 179, 180, 182
Riel, Marguerite, *née* Monet *dit* Bellehumeur (wife), *104*, 110-115, 121, 135, 143-146, 181, 184; marriage, 112, 181
Riel, Marie (sister), 12, 14, 32, 80, 82, 167, 180; death, 85, 176
Riel, Marie-Angélique (daughter), *104*, 115, 135, 143, 145, 147, 149, 181, 182
Riel, Octavie (sister), 12, 14, 31, 80, 106, 167, 180
Riel, Sara (sister), 7, 8, 10, 12-14, 29, 32, 78, 80, 85, 97, 107, 113, 166, 180; missionary nun, 169, 175; death, 116, 182
Riel family, 12, 25, 33, 80, 91, 101, 106, 110, 163, 167
Riel farm, 1, 41, 82, 83, 167, 175
Ritchot, Father Noël-Joseph, 32, 44, 45, 62, 68, 70, 71, 81
Ritchot, Janvier, 4, 70

River Road, 1
Rivière Sale, 48
Rocky Point, 112, 181
Ross, James, 54, 55, 57, 61
Roy, Dr. François, 102, 140
Rupert's Land, 30, 42, 57, 58, 159, 160, 164, 165, 171

Saskatchewan River, 47, 69
Saskatchewan territory, 71, 85, 107, 109, 116, 117, 124, 131, 140, 166, 175, 180, 182, 183
Sault St. Louis, 20
Saulteaux People, 2, 9, 175, 176, 177, 178
Sayer, Pierre-Guillaume, 11, 166
Schmidt, Louis, 15, 18, 20, 33-35, 42, 58, 73, 80, 122, 124, 168, 169
Schulz, John, 34, 44, 57, 62, 65, 66, 70, 79, 83, 89, 174
Scott, Alfred, 14, 62
Scott, Thomas, 65, 67, 73, 76, 85, 87, 115, 122, 151, 153, 174
Scott affair, 70-73, 83, 87, 176
Scottish settlers, 9, 161, 162
Scrip, 177, 181
Seine River, 7, 8, 11, 163, 167
Selkirk colonists, 161, 162, 168
separate schools, 68, 69
Sioux People, 8, 15, 109, 131, 179
Sitting Bull, 109, 179, 180
Smith, Donald, 59, 60, 62, 66, 67
Snow, John, 42, 45, 172
South Saskatchewan River, 115
South Saskatchewan River Valley, 182
St. Anthony, 30
St. Boniface, 9, 12, 80, 82, 165, 168, 169, 175
St. Boniface Cathedral, 13, 28, 29, 43, 48, 169, 172
St. Boniface College, 106

Stewart, James, 73
St. Joseph, 30, 78, 80, 175, 180
St. Laurent, 125, 128, 129, 183
St. Lawrence River, 20
St. Norbert, 32, 45, 47, 85, 173
St. Patrick's Church, 93
St. Paul, 17, 30, 41, 42, 69, 83, 89, 106, 143, 171, 175, 177, 180
St. Peter's Mission, 114, 181
St. Vital, 30, 79, 80, 85, 100, 115, 143, 171, 175, 181
Sun River, 114, 115
Suncook, 95, 96
surveyors, 1, 3, 4, 42-47, 172, 173
Swan, Joseph, 114

Tabor, Corporal (guard), 144, 145, 149
Taché, Archbishop A.A., 12, 13, 20, 25, 68, 73, 78, 83, 84, 101, 115, 165, 166, 168, 175, 179
Tourond, Baptiste, 3

United States, 8, 47, 53, 70, 79, 87, 101, 143, 159-161, 163-166, 169, 170, 171, 172, 173, 175,177-182
Upper Canada, 9, 36, 160, 164
Upper Fort Garry. *See* Fort Garry

Valade, Dr. F.X., 147, 148
voyageurs, 2, 47, 69, 73, 162

Washington, D.C., 90, 92, 93, 177, 178, 182
Winnipeg, 30, 31, 35, 57, 65, 66, 82, 114, 143, 176
Wolseley, Colonel Garnet, 70, 76, 77, 78, 125, 155, 174, 175
Wood Mountain, 109, 180
Worcester, 95

York Factory, 47